EMERGENCY MESSAGES

EMERGENCY MESSAGES

An Autobiographical Miscellany

CARL SOLOMON

EDITED AND WITH A FOREWORD BY

JOHN TYTELL

PARAGON HOUSE
New York

First edition, 1989

Published in the United States by

Paragon House Publishers
90 Fifth Avenue
New York, NY 10011

Copyright © 1989 by Paragon House Publishers

Manufactured in the United States of America

Library of Congress Cataloging-in-Publication Data

Solomon, Carl, 1928–
Emergency messages: an autobiographical miscellany/
by Carl Solomon;
edited and with a foreword by John Tytell—1st ed.
p. cm.
Contents: The messengerial revolution—An interview with Carl Solomon—Carl's story—Sanity and the sanitarium—Emergency messages—Beat reflections—Epistles—Fugitive poems—Reviews.
ISBN 1-55778-122-2   ISBN 1-55778-178-8 (pbk.)
1. Solomon, Carl, 1928– —Biography. 2. Authors, American—20th century—Biography. 3. Psychiatric hospital patients—United States—Biography. 4. Bohemianism—United States. I. Tytell, John. II. Title.
PS3569.O6Z465   1988
818.5409—dc19
[B]   88-10232
CIP

dedicated to Alfred Jarry

"The pure products of America go crazy"
William Carlos Williams

CONTENTS

THE COMEDIAN AS COMMON DENOMINATOR

Carl Solomon is known as the dedicatee of "Howl," the most famous long poem written by an American since T.S. Eliot's "The Waste Land." Eliot's mosaic masterpiece was dedicated to Ezra Pound, his friend and collaborator ("*il miglior fabbro*": the greater craftsman). Ginsberg's dedication may be more spiritually motivated than that of Eliot, who was acknowledging the ruthless excisions that Pound proposed to shape the poem. Eliot had written much of his poem in a Swiss sanitarium while recovering from a nervous breakdown; he was perennially unsure of himself and uncertain about the possibility that what he had written was merely therapeutic. When he submitted his manuscript to Pound, the most confident literary figure of the moment, Pound immediately recognized the poem's universal appeal.

Carl Solomon was less the mentor and more the inspiring friend. The prominent part he plays in the now published annotations to "Howl" suggests how much of it reflects his acts and anecdotes. In 1949 Carl Solomon had been in the New York Psychiatric Institute at Columbia Presbyterian Hospital for two months when he met Allen Ginsberg, who had been remanded there in lieu of facing felony charges stemming from a fracas involving a stolen car in which he was a passenger. Six years earlier, Solomon had begun his studies at City College and Ginsberg his at Columbia University. Going through a Marxist phase, Solomon joined the American Youth for Democracy, a leftist organization known as the Tom Paine Club. His inquisitive nature caused him to begin shipping out on merchant marine vessels after the war. In 1947 he jumped ship in France and made his way to Paris, searching for Surrealists and Existentialists (called "excrementalists" by some of the French then). He found a copy of Henry Miller's *Black Spring* in a bookstall on the Seine, and he read it, fascinated by Miller's ebullience—*"C'est pour rire, pas pour lire"*—for laughing, not for reading, he was told by a Frenchman in a bar—but he found more of Miller's books. One day he witnessed an Artaud reading in Saint-Germain-des-Prés. He became interested in Artaud's book, *Van Gogh, The Man Suicided by Society*, in which Artaud condemned all psychiatry, claiming that most mental patients were gifted with a lucidity that allowed them to see through social shams. When he returned to New York, Solomon was in a very negative, nihilistic state, thinking about suicide and lobotomy. Reading Gide's *Lafcadio's Adventures*, he became intrigued by the idea of gratuitous crime, stole a sandwich from the Brooklyn College cafeteria, where he had transferred, disowning his left wing entanglements. He admitted his theft to a guard, and was then sent to Psychiatric Institute.

Almost as soon as Ginsberg arrived at Psychiatric Institute, he met Carl Solomon. Ginsberg was nervous, anxious to be assigned to a room, wondering what it would be like to live with a group of men who were supposed to be crazy. The tension of facing criminal indictment had made him unsure of his own grip on reality. When he entered his ward he saw a large man being wheeled in on a stretcher. Emerging from an insulin shock coma, Solomon asked Ginsberg, in a literate tone, who he was. Testing Solomon's sensibility, Ginsberg answered that he was Prince Myshkin, the saintly character in Dostoyevski's *The Idiot*. Solomon retorted that he was Kirilov, the suicidal nihilist in *The Possessed* who is unable to tolerate any signs of ecstasy. The characterization was respectively apt, defining a continuing tension in their friendship. They met freely on the ward for several months, writing imaginary letters to figures like T.S. Eliot and reading aloud to each other. Ginsberg read Yeats and Melville and told Solomon about his friends Kerouac and Burroughs. Solomon introduced Ginsberg to his favorite French surrealists, Michaux, Isou, Artaud, and also Genet. Ginsberg took notes on Solomon's curious adventures and his aphoristic exclamations.

The two young men had different expectations of the role of the writer. Solomon characterized Ginsberg as a "dopey daffodil" because Ginsberg seemed to represent a Wordsworthian projection of sensitivity rather than Artaud's surrealist conception of the poet as brute. In Psychiatric Institute, Ginsberg seemed entirely conventional with a neat haircut and horn-rimmed glasses. The two friends fought continually over every intellectual and aesthetic point: Ginsberg, for example, saw Whitman as a sexual revolutionary, and Solomon argued that his political ideas were more important. They also disputed the relative merits of the psychoanalysts: Solomon was being analyzed by a woman, a disciple of Harry Stack Sullivan, and Ginsberg by a Freudian. Ginsberg described the doctors in a letter to Jack Kerouac as "ghouls of mediocrity," claiming that the staff interpreted absurd or eccentric actions as madness. According to novelist John Clellon Holmes, Ginsberg's analyst was soon left confused and completely at a loss, feeling that his patient was saner and surely more honest than he was.

Released from Psychiatric Institute, Ginsberg began to introduce Solomon to some of his other friends. He persuaded Carl to rent a cold-water flat on 17th Street where they held a New Year's Eve party. Ginsberg introduced Solomon to Jay Landesman, a patron of the arts from St. Louis who edited a magazine called *Neurotica*, one of the earliest postwar publications to anticipate the sexual revolution. Landesman would print both Ginsberg's and Solomon's work. Solomon began contributing book reviews to *The New Leader* and worked as an editor for his uncle, A.A. Wyn, the publisher of Ace Books. In 1952, William Burroughs sent installments of the manuscript of *Junky*, a realistic account of the life of the drug addict, to Ginsberg in New York. Ginsberg showed the material to Solomon, who helped get the book published by Ace, the first of any of the Beat books to appear in print.

Solomon later would have two of his own books published by City Lights Press, *Mishaps, Perhaps* and *More Mishaps*. The books are comprised of staccato routines, strange anecdotes, and pithy essays, all reflecting Solomon's self-imposed and quixotic role of the world's intellectual antagonist. Called the "lunatic saint" by his friends, Solomon would fulfill their expectations by performing all kinds of weird acts: the perfectly Dadaist gesture of throwing potato salad at novelist Wallace Markfield who was lecturing on Mallarmé, an act commemorated in "Howl"; pretending to be W.H. Auden at an exhibition and gleefully signing autographs in Auden's name; driving up to Ossining to sit in a car outside Sing Sing prison while the Rosenbergs were executed; selling ice cream in front of the United Nations after leaving his position as an editor for Ace Books. "Every man lives by a set of rules to which he is the only exception," Solomon once wrote. To Ginsberg, Solomon was an instance of the artist as outrage, a man capable of an intuitively quick surrealistic buffoonery that exposed the pretentious stuffiness of the world. Like Ginsberg, Solomon was an outcast artist, an exile within the culture.

Carl Solomon spent the years from 1956 to 1964 as an inmate at Pilgrim State Hospital in Brentwood, Long Island. At that time, it was the largest mental institution in the world, with 25,000 patients. Ginsberg, whose mother Naomi had received a frontal lobotomy at the same hospital, has acknowledged that Carl's commitment triggered the composition of "Howl." Psychiatry, mental institutions, psychic breakdowns may one day be regarded as a key to understanding the artists of our era. And the madness of outrage has not been limited in our time to the Beats: witness the lives of Robert Lowell, John Berryman, Theodore Roethke, Delmore Schwartz, Sylvia Plath—all cases of beleaguered writers unable to bear the realities of the world. Lowell, writing to John Berryman in March 1959, seemed to offer a touchstone for the age when he complained of "something curiously twisted and against the grain about the world poets of my generation have to live in."

Carl Solomon, in his "Report From the Asylum," claimed that he had been conditioned in his illness by classical surrealism. In the years after the First World War, the French Surrealists had used art as a means of protesting the social inequities they opposed, and their style flaunted the bizarre and absurd. As the French photographer Henri Cartier-Bresson has observed, Surrealism was a revolt in *life* as well as art, but surrealist presentation could easily be misinterpreted as madness. This was the case of Antonin Artaud, the French dramatist with whom Solomon identified. Artaud, who ultimately died in the madhouse, passionately denounced psychiatry as an agency of social conditioning. Artaud claimed the honest insights of so-called lunatics were intolerable to society. Instead of burning them at the medieval stake as witches, they were encouraged to conform with shock treatments and tranquilizers. For his part, Carl Solomon received seventy-one insulin or electroshock treatments during his years of psychiatric confinement. While in certain phases the comparison to Artaud seems valid, in Solomon's more vulnerable states there seems to be an even greater affinity with the condition that Franz Kafka created for his victimized characters in *The Castle* and *The Trial*. Solomon was introduced to Kafka as a young man (by Samuel Schoenbaum, now known as a Shakespeare scholar, then a student renting a room from Carl's mother in Parkchester in the Bronx) and identified with what he read. At one moment, Kafka's central figure—who does not even deserve a proper name—can be seen vehement, enraged, proudly strutting; suddenly, without explanation, he is cowering, pleading, fearing a fly in the room, somehow soiled, degraded and dehumanized by his terrors. In "Report From the Asylum," Solomon investigates this Kafkian situation as it can be caused by bureaucratically imposed conditions of coma. It is a harrowing inquiry into the "succubus" of shock which would transform anyone's view of the world: "my body, insulin-packed, would become to me an enormous concrete pun with infinite levels of association." The ensuing state shifts from a timeless sense of being everywhere simultaneously to the transcendence of earthly considerations, then panic, amnesia, the Void. The experience seems to approximate our understanding of death, and Solomon becomes a sort of Lazarus returned from an underworld.

Like Franz Kafka, who only published four stories in his lifetime and who ordered his friend Max Brod to burn all his extant writing, Carl Solomon has been a writer without apparent ambitions. He has been one of the marginal underground intellectuals of our moment and his writing has appeared in fugitive magazines like *Neurotica*, *Oink* or *Exquisite Corpse*. His work exists as a sort of literary graffiti. His particular perspective is that civilization is a joke, that integrity is our supreme fiction, and that truth is blurred and often relative to power. In a piece on Artaud he states that we live in a generation of "charlatanry, propaganda and corruption, and that there is no room for an honest man on either side of the Iron Curtain." Like Artaud, he argues that most language is merely babble, and that sometimes it would be better to chew bubble gum. While there may be a certain incongruity in such a position, for a writer at least, it does seem related to Samuel Beckett's world as it is defined by its silences and its distrust of language as a means of communication.

Solomon's stance in this no-man's place of muted despair is a bare minimalism and an aggressive comedy.

The minimalism is seen in the terse compactness of his expression, a rapid, shorthand definition that often seems elliptical or surrealist in genealogy. Solomon is not even so much an essayist as he is a miniaturist, microscopically searching for human signs in an alien landscape. What saves his vision from Beckett's bleakness is the quality of his antic humor, a delight in the ordinary even as the banal provokes outrageous gesture when it becomes boring or repetitive. So Solomon the wise becomes the wise-guy, the comedian as common denominator, and his writing becomes animated by the barbs and quips that serve as a protection in an unfriendly world. He sees himself not as the "distinguished poet but the extinguished one"; he says reading is a means of preventing masturbation; he proposes to overthrow the government through farce and violins; he notes that he does not desire to become President, but only absolute dictator with a palace in Kansas built of butter-crunch candy. Like Artaud who knew how to use a hard shell of nonsense to avoid fruitless rational discourse, Solomon's humor often seems an inadequate defense system, the register of a sensibility struggling to cope with vastly superior forces. And when he is very serious, his views often are unorthodox and unsettling. A quarter of a century ago, in an unnervingly understated manner, he pointed to a central domestic debility: "The tendency toward crime among the young men of my generation is impossible to surmount." And on a broader social scale he has suggested that there is little difference between those inside and outside mental institutions. Such views may seem eccentric and unfashionable, but on a deeper level they remind us that Carl Solomon has existed as one of the sensitive antennae of our age.

John Tytell

I
THE
MESSENGERIAL
REVOLUTION

This era is so confusing that I don't know where to begin or whom to blame for the troubles besetting me. The wrongs done me have been too many and have often been too obscene in nature for me to recount. Most of them I would surmise have been inspired by jealousy of either my physical or intellectual prowess. Both of which have generally been considerable. Only last Sunday I completed all three puzzles on the newspaper puzzle page flawlessly. Then, on the way home from my daily visit to my mother in a nursing home, I sat down on a bench at the bus-stop. There was a black fisherman wearing a Mets cap sitting beside me. I too wear a Mets cap. A school bus carrying Puerto Rican children came tearing by. "Faggot," they screamed. The black fisherman held out an extended finger at the departing bus, in a returned obscene gesture. Then we discussed flounder fishing. I warned him to beware of fish and game wardens enforcing the new 8-inch flounder law. "How do I know you're not a fish and game warden?" he asked. Taken aback, I shut up.

It's very hard to take, but I hang in there. There are bright spots here and there: a good blood pressure reading, my tax man finding some figures in my favor, my coming up with an answer to a difficult trivia question. But in most cases there is continual backbiting and a general greyness or somberness hanging over my life. I sometimes find myself unwittingly identifying with the protagonist of Dostoyevski's *Notes From The Underground*. What a sad life I lead!

My shortcomings are so glaring that I no longer know how to hide them. With my mother gone many problems of household management arise. I am obliged to run terrified to neighbors asking them how to defrost a refrigerator, how to obtain a paint job from the landlord, how to use the stove, et cetera ad infinitum. I have never learned to be resourceful and now I am finally left on my own. Well, I had been on my own once upon a time, but that is too long past to dwell on now—the days when I had been a beatnik running around the city trying to be hip and cool, to cope, to infiltrate, to adjust, to break the silver cord, or whatever term we used at any given moment to describe what we were trying to do. Ages ago!

In those youthful years, I nearly ruined my health, really knowing very little about the subject. In recent years, inspired by an old college friend, I have become something of a health nut. But in this realm also, for every type of bandaid I apply to my anatomy, a new, undreamed of plague rears its head in the next morning's banner type.

The news is confusing. Take Reagan. Is he Irish? Is he Catholic or Protestant? The media are never quite specific. All I know is that he is against the Evil Empire and he is not Jewish. And take the situation in Cambodia. Are we backing the Khmer Rouge against the Heng Samrin people? Who are the good guys and who are the bad guys? Can't tell the players without a scorecard. Are the Khmer Rouge good now? Who's on first?

Today is Passover, so I yielded to pressure from my Jewish neighbors and stayed home from work. Last week I had been asked to read a poem by Artaud for some surrealist organization—a poem in which Artaud requests respite from judgments by the Deity. I said I could not read it because its thrust is atheistic and at present I am somewhat involved with my local Jewish congregation. Contradictions everywhere, but in most cases mercenary motives hold final sway. The Almighty Buck?

Artaud wrote that all writing is pigshit. Ought Artaudians keep silent? Did Artaud keep silent after writing those words or did he continue writing—self-labeled pigshit? Do words, written or uttered mean anything whatsoever? In just this period, 1987, I would state without a doubt that one should suspect every written utterance one encounters of being hypocritical. Things are just so *chancy* nowadays. Where then are the youth to look for guidance, if not to literary works of their day? By all means I would urge them to search for meaning only in the school of experience.

Allen Ginsberg's answering machine spoke in his own voice last night when I called and it sounded very weary (I think of a pun: Lord Weary's Castle). I'll try him again later today. I plan to visit my mother at the nursing home and perhaps to drop in at the shul.

Some time has passed since my last writing, a couple of days. Days of work. I work as a messenger. After nearly five years I have it down to a fine art. No cheating on the job; I am very conscientious. I know the Wall Street area thoroughly by this time—from the porn palace to the eateries to the best places to sit for a moment to the place where, in the summertime, one can participate in a trivia contest to the places where one can buy *The Nation* or find shelter during a downpour. I finished early yesterday, but today's paper has pictures of Wall Streeters arrested yesterday afternoon for coke dealing. They were led out of the office buildings manacled together. Sorry I missed it. It must have occurred (the bust) after I'd finished my day.

We're off today, Wall Street being closed up for Good Friday. A chance to catch up with things befitting a man of my years. I am expecting a call from a young lawyer about a will I have decided to draw up. Having no children, I am leaving my assets to organizations. Cultural and political. May I apply to myself the term PHILANTHROPIST? Of course, after deduction is made for my burial, I would also like a fairly impressive memorial stone. Nothing, of course, to rival Shah Jehan. Just something to indicate that I have been a writer and an editor. Perhaps "thinker" would be enough. But that would be too eccentric in this day and age.

Abbie Hoffman, whom I met five years ago and who impressed me as perhaps the Jewish Fidel Castro, is leading a demonstration in Washington today. I am off from work. Too rainy for fishing. This seems exactly, *but exactly*, like the sixties when I was still here, at this very desk writing those two books of mine, *Mishaps, Perhaps* and *More Mishaps*. All that is missing is the late poet, Harry Fainlight, now dead.

Harry, once considered a most promising British poet, had cultivated me shortly after I left Pilgrim State Hospital in the sixties. He'd recited to me his Spider poem (his most famous work) and later broken off with me in an angry letter because I'd been timorous about visiting him in his room in Chatham Square on the edge of Chinatown.

Really I am forced to the conclusion that the serious developments of my time, intellectual and political, occurred during the years right after the war and that the rest of this is a continual repetitious run-off from that scenario.

Some time back I heard the phrase, "Hoss is Boss" referring to heroin addiction. Are tranquilizers boss in my case? I am still taking mellaril 31 years after my "breakdown"—though my dose has been cut to what is now termed "a fly's dose."

I would be the last person to complain about this situation, I who played with the idea of suicide at twenty. I have devoured dozens of delicious Belgian waffles since that year and my taste-buds say, "No. Life in whatever form is preferable to suicide."

It was some time back that Elaine and I began going out together, just after I'd been released from Pilgrim State and I'd decided to resurrect the concept of the high school romance, with dating, Valentine cards and the rest of it. Back in the sixties, when we also read *A Man And A Maid* together and Elaine was interested in Bob Dylan, Charles Aznavour, and Joe Orton. So yesterday we saw together, still on the Upper West Side which she inhabits, the movie on Joe Orton's life and murder, *Prick Up Your Ears*. It felt really good to see the sixties from a retrospective angle. She'd been trying to help me to adjust to normal life after hospitalization. We reaped the fruits of our labours yesterday, together in "normal" society 23 years after my release. Success of a kind. Not in the conventional sense, seeing one's name in lights. However, success of a subtler kind, basking in one's freedom from straitjackets and bars 23 years later. Maybe it's time to try for conventional success. Do I have the energy at 59?

Today, I and the home attendant will probably attempt to wash my uncle's hair. He sure needs it. It will be a struggle, probably accompanied by yells and screams. I will also visit my mother at the nursing home. We're lucky to have the elderly to help cushion us against the shock of imminent mortality.

I have been reading a book on Cicero. Why? Because of aging. When I was a young student I studied Cicero in a Latin class with the help of an interlinear translation—and so flagrant was my use of the translation, known as a "pony," that my classmates dubbed me "Pony Boy" (not praise). O tempora, O mores and on thru Catiline's conspiracy, the entire thing comes alive to me as I read through the biography of Cicero. I never could quite identify Catiline's brand of evil in modern terms and still cannot, as Cicero thunderously invokes virtue against him. Perhaps the Manson crew of the sixties is as close to Catiline's conspiracy as we can come in modern terms. But again, why Cicero? Because in his Tusculan Disputations there is one oration called *De Senectute* (his philosophy of growing older and facing death) which I had translated with the aid of the pony in high school and which I feel has relevance to my present state.

I see in Cicero a tranquil acceptance of death, seeing it as something good, freedom for the soul. We were dealing with these eternal verities when we were kids in schools for bright boys (no girls then) but were more involved in competition and showing off our smartness rather than in digesting the wisdom we were working with. The background, however, comes in handy now. What if I'd never read Cicero? I'd have to fall back on Ann Landers or something.

"And someday you may even doubt your own existence," asserted Teddy Goodman, my short story class teacher at City College in 1943. I was then fifteen years old and a freshman in college. How clairvoyant Goodman was I was still to learn, but I certainly did experience just the writer's fate that he was describing when I reached twenty-seven, had broken up with my wife and was supporting myself in a furnished room on the West Side with a publishing job. In addition to seeing a Washington School therapist. In fact, that became, for a while, the crux of my problems—to assure myself that I existed. To be a writer you must suffer. I can accept this now, having duly suffered. Now I am enjoying some kind of reward, writing without a great career stake, almost a senior citizen, at the brink of retirement age, with all of that suffering to look back upon painlessly. The part that seems most painful to me, as I recollect in tranquility (Wordsworthian) is the agony of smoking and coughing, the inexorable addiction I suffered from during most of my youth. I have not smoked for three years and my lungs are clear, my appetite is good, and my sense of smell (long deadened) has been restored. Unfortunately I did not stop quite soon enough because there is early emphysema which is not reversible. But the gain in stopping was considerable. I go rowing at City Island because rowing is a highly recommended exercise for emphysemiacs. At twenty-two, I was trying hard to play the role of a young writer in the Village and smoking cigarettes was part of the pose. Beat writer John Clellon Holmes, who was a role model to me then, later developed a devastating mouth cancer, but at that time helped to create the image of the anxious, chain-smoking, existentialist-era writer. He even coined the phrase, "the nervous puff." The health-destroying pose has been revealed for what it was. Even then, that pose was an antidote to another pose, the pseudo-healthy pose of wartime Stalinism. So the nervous pose, in its own time, also had a genuine raison d'etre.

Two rather unpleasant weeks of feuding with J. at home and Mr. Q. on the job. J. is a retired man who stands guard with his dog outside my apartment house almost continually and involves himself in all one's affairs. He becomes abusive if you do not take his advice. Q. is a tall, thin Auschwitz survivor who regards all gentiles as anti-Semites and takes me to task for not agreeing with him. I become annoyed with him occasionally and become abusive of him every once in a while. When these feuds are going, they drive out of your head all more pleasant thoughts and require all your intellectual energy to keep them from flowing over into violence.

These minor feuds convince me of the enormous complexity of all human relationships and the impossibility of straightening things out on an international or world political level. I remember during the sixties when Allen Ginsberg was involved in the peace movement and fights among his friends broke out occasionally at the farm in Cherry Valley, he commented: "How can we bring peace to the world when we can't even bring it to our own household?"

There are "ghosts" like TV ghosts in my mind. For example, I may be involved in some activity of the immediate present and I will suddenly visualize in my mind's eye, very graphically as to physical detail, the entire world of Pilgrim State Hospital: Steckrider the attendant, Gruschka, the Russian who made ceramics in OT, Pegmum, Garfield Turner, or Chester, the decayed old man. I may suddenly visualize the world of Fountainhouse, the mental patients' club on the west side of Manhattan as I remember it in the late fifties, when Elvis was riding high (and Mickey Mantle). These ghastly memories blend into the present mood and form one's fabric of awareness. Stephen King moods and Muppet moods float gently by in the atmosphere in wait for a passerby to wander into them. The fact that I experienced the mental illness phenomenon so early in life is the reason I have been left to toss the issue around for so many subsequent decades. It's not as though I had passed a full career as, say, a merchant seaman, or even as a book maven. I (and Allen Ginsberg, with whom I've been in rather steady contact) have been ex-mental patients for nearly forty years now.

Elisa and I have made plans to go to Orchard Beach over the Memorial Day weekend. The scene should be vaguely reminiscent of Celine's Robinson in *Voyage Au Bout De La Nuit*. She is a big, lusty girl, a former patient whom I met in the neighborhood and we have been having a very satisfactory romance for about a year now. She first met my mother one day when I was out fishing and my mother mentioned she had a son. Eliza took it from there.

The neighbors have divided into two camps: pro- and anti-cat. Some are in favor of the group of cats we have in the basement remaining and others want them driven out. One of the cats was driven into some kind of chute and seems still to be living there. This conflict among the neighbors brings torrents of highly emotional abuse exchanged in notes Scotch-taped to the elevator wall. "Sadist—I will break both your arms if I find you—you have maimed a cat." Et cetera.

Most of the men in the building are quite proficient mechanically. I am less so. This adds to my difficulties.

Fifty-nine years of life, I feel, qualify me to be a connoisseur of world drama. I feel, perhaps incorrectly since another century of life would give me a better perspective, that the first half of our twentieth century somehow resonated with mightier footfalls than its second half has. Do Castro and Khomeini, Reagan and Gorbachev, Carter and Marcos, Sadat and Idi Amin quite measure up to Roosevelt and Churchill, Pétain and Rommel, Mussolini and Chamberlain? Perhaps I oughtn't to forget that there were humorists and satirists and caricaturists in those days too who could make the major figures of those times seem insignificant or ridiculous also. And then, too, I did not witness as my mother and father did, the century's beginnings. To my mother, who still remembers Taft as the president with the big belly, the century seems splayed out as one flat surface, without high points or low points and with the actors on its stage to be judged by the same standards (Wilson was a dreamer, Roosevelt was good, the best, Eisenhower was always busy playing golf). In my poor father's mind—he died in '39—Gabriele D'Annunzio occupied the same role as Patton or MacArthur do in so many American (particularly veteran) minds today.

Orators. My reference to Cicero above probably betrays a hidden interest in oratory I have often harbored. This had its origin in a stammering, stuttering series of brief speech disorders I suffered from as a child. I was a "nervous" child and so a good prospect for a "Howl" dedication even in those days. Anyway my father cited to me the great orator Demosthenes as an example to follow in overcoming the speech defects. Demosthenes was famous for filling his mouth with pebbles to cure himself of stammering. If he stammered with pebbles in his mouth, he might swallow one and die. The great emphasis here was placed on willpower (not always favored by anxiety-combating modern psychiatrists). I recently stopped smoking through the old-fashioned method of "willpower" and it has worked for over three years. It probably has no substitute in achieving results.

When I think of role models of the old hip era, I think not of Kerouac, as so many hippie types seem to, nor of Neal Cassady as Kesey admirers seem to, but of Stanley Gould, the noncreative apostle of heterosexuality (you needed "apostles of heterosexuality" in those days, honest to God). When I gave up Dada and got married in 1950, Stanley seemed to have something cerebral to offer me as a substitute and that was the low-cost, piquant, literary hip bohemian moral code. Stanley was really a symbol of this to insiders (though Kerouac tried to do this for a mass audience at times) and such paternal advice was much called for by those of us in our twenties at that time. By now I've given up some of it but some of hip discipline remains. Something like Hemingway's "grace under pressure." For a while we were a brave little heterosexual group in 181 Prince Street where Olive and I had sublet an apartment from Anatole Broyard. Stanley and a little hip group from Waterbury, Connecticut lived directly above us and I would count the first half of this period to be about the happiest of my life.

Gouldiana: Stanley had a reputation for short, terse utterance. Once he'd been busted and Allen Ginsberg met him on the street a short time afterward. Allen asked what had happened. Stanley's reply was simply: "SS"—suspended sentence. According to Anatole Broyard's "Portrait Of The Hipster," he was given to making "metonymous gestures" and to seeking "eleemosynary." He remarked to me at various times that he had never worked a day in his life and also that he'd "never been a john" (never patronized a whore).

As Olive and I became alienated from each other, the early pleasure faded. But there is still a green patch in my memory for that brief interlude of self-styled bohemian living. We all supported ourselves with little, short-term jobs and, I suppose, secretly lusted after luxury. But now that I have tasted a bit of it (luxury), I have nothing but nostalgia for the hip past with its semi-poverty and bohemian defiance. Those days when one took a job principally in the hope of receiving unemployment compensation, and when one never stayed at a job long enough to earn a vacation.

Sex is always an interesting subject to approach and attitudes toward the erotic tend to be cyclical. Nowadays, with AIDS awareness in such vogue, I amuse myself with thoughts about erotic attitudes in eras past. About sixteen or seventeen years after my father had been describing me to strangers as a potential "chip off the old block" (a carbon copy of him, buckaroo of the twenties) I was being initiated to sexual attitudes aboard ship that had nothing in common with anything I ever discussed with Allen Ginsberg in later years but which was part of a store of information that was then only beginning to amass. The connection of sex to money was an extremely close one and one's virility or attractiveness depended on whether one paid for one's intercourse or whether it was granted "for love." Practically undreamed of, but still within the realm of the imaginable was the possibility of being paid oneself for one's favors by a woman. Homosexuality and its variety of roles soon connected conversationally with this. The whole hustler mentality was not far removed from the sailor mentality and, believe it or not, the bourgeois business of making lucrative matches, practiced in the Borscht Belt as well as among European royal houses, is not more than a nuance or two away. Anthropological attitudes toward sex and varying conceptions of good or evil connected with sex flow in infinite profusion from these early discoveries. Literature, Whitman, Genet, Eliot, Lawrence, *Neurotica*, Kerouaciana, and almost all the conversation among my peers during the Beat era, were concerned with a dissection of the role of the erotic in the various power and survival struggles of life. And on into the AIDS era. I notice that younger kids are unfamiliar nowadays with the term "bulldagger" and older folks (like me) find strange talk of, say, fist-fucking. This is only one example. The one constant is the fact that erotic expertise in any era is generally confused, sometimes second hand and, always unreliable. It is the fun, not the wisdom, of an era.

Today, I saw *Predator* with Elisa. Apart from its being an obvious intentional successor to *The Terminator* as a vehicle for the wondrous Arnold Schwartzenegger, it is the first genuine throwback to the 1930s type of war film I was brought up on that I have seen in the modern era. Here are heroes utterly devoid of ambiguity or any observable inner life fighting and dying in amicable and heroic masculine companionship much like the heroic and physically formidable cowboys of my boyhood. The all-male cast (no homosexual tinge) with the lone woman acceptable as "one of the guys." These are heroes generations removed from the draftee-types of Sgt. Bilko films, more akin to either the mercenary or sheer adventurer types. This seems an attempt to give a new generation the notion that war is pleasurable. Even that death on a battlefield assumes a blissful aspect. All we need now is another war and more John Clellon Holmeses psychoanalyzing popular culture after that war. Doesn't anything really new ever happen?

Once more, I think of past times—now of the Yorkshire Residence Hotel, so well described by Joyce Johnson, and the events immediately preceding my incarceration in Pilgrim State Hospital. In the Yorkshire were a group of presumably simpatico young intellectuals with a generally socialist and psychological orientation. These were at that time not the post-war hip element to be found in the Village, but a younger, more academically grounded group coming of age during the McCarthy (Joseph, not Eugene) era. One of the most dramatic events during that Yorkshire stay lingers in my memory—a whole group of us driving by car up to Ossining on the night of the Rosenberg executions and sitting in the parked car on an

Ossining street until, by the watch of one of the occupants of the car, the Rosenbergs had been executed. The moods generated by that atmosphere had me bouncing between the ideas of a Jehovah Witness proselytizer named Bob Savage and the psychological insights of Don Cook, a friend of Allen's. During this period, too, I edited Burroughs' first book, *Junky*. I was in a sort of non-directive psychotherapy at that time, toying with Zen ideas and floundering socially after a recent divorce. I would spend nights swilling beer with a social group led by a man named Williamson who described himself as "a male lesbian" whose taste in women ran to lesbic types who flocked to his apartment. Gender differences were becoming somewhat confusing for me and reached a kind of climax when two unhinging encounters occurred: (a) I took to bed a secretary from my office who turned out to have a distended clitoris—a small penis—and (b) I was accosted near Central Park—while walking home from work, not cruising—by a white man of some education who requested that I urinate in his mouth. I later referred to him as the Central Park Masochist. He was wearing a red beret, a couple of decades before the Guardian Angels and at my tender age (about 26) I was quite shaken up. Not only that, but I had just come across a book called *The Philosophy of a Lunatic* which supplanted the Zen interest with the desire to become "a professional Lunatic." On the way to Pilgrim State, where a group of us were sent after processing at Bellevue, we resembled the bad boys from "Pinocchio" on a fool's vacation to Funland. Among my fellow patients on that strange ride, which ensued after hastily vacating the Yorkshire, was the one-time columnist for the *World-Telegram*, Ray Brock—by then a ceaselessly laughing and apparently seriously deteriorated alcoholic. The Pilgrim era defies description even in retrospect and even in the wake of subsequent amazing vistas and adventures. We formed friendships, were herded into the many buildings; we were generally jovial and glad to get regular food again; we were eager to know what was going on in a world which seemed to be shaken to its roots with the death of Stalin, the Castro Revolution in Cuba, pot paranoia, red scare, the Algerian War, Dien Bien Phu, and peripheral Armageddon expectation. What a period that! Things do slow down though and there are plateaus as well as precipices.

When I first came to making messengering my occupation during the recession of the early eighties, I thought naturally of Henry Miller's writing on the subject. I had never read *The Tropic of Capricorn* though *Cancer* had long been one of my favorites. I immediately went to a bookstore and bought a copy of *Capricorn*. It painted a nightmarish picture of life at "The Cosmodynamic Messenger Service." Miller had been a dispatcher and I was farther down in the hierarchy. In my mind's eye, I had another self-image than the Millerian one, though I am a writer too. I identified with an aging bachelor my mother and I had met in an Adirondack summer resort during the forties. He had spoken of himself as "working on Wall Street," which turned out to be a euphemism for messengering. To me, he, rather than the rowdy, anarchistic Miller became my role model for this period of my life. I began sending things out to mags about the subtle charms of being a middle-aged messenger, the joy of being semi-retired, a little marginal and not quite in the main stream of workaday life. The general atmosphere, though, was very much in the Millerian vein, full of subtly ironic moments involving the joys and tragedies of young boys, aging men, crazies, fugitives, and mongolian idiots (part of a program to break them into a working life). There were a sprinkling of poets, writers, and off-beat types of all races and nationalities, refugees from tyranny and psychologically-bruised potential tyrants. Another departure from the Miller mold, was the entry of a trade union into the picture. This was complicated, involving the Teamsters, who brought us paid vacations in addition to the alleged Teamster connection with the mob. All the conflicts in this area, as of this writing, are not yet completely resolved. However, there is here the down-to-earth *Germinal* and Odetsian quality mingling with elements of *The Wild Duck* and *La Folle De Chaillot*.

The most boring summer of my life was the summer of 1981, when I was working as a cashier in B. Dalton's bookstore and the bulk of our customers were into buying Rubik's cubes. We had just been through the Reagan-Hinckley-Haig excitement and the Rubik's cubes fad came as an extraordinarily dulling weight upon my sensibilities. That and other factors (like my mother's falling into senility and my terrible cough from cigarettes) created a horrible atmosphere for me, in which I eventually lost that job for "substandard performance." The Kerouac Conference in Boulder in '82 with its inspiring vistas of Rocky Mountain peaks started me back on the road to a kind of resuscitation involving giving up smoking and getting Mom into a *good* nursing home. The chaos at Dalton's was epitomized by the firm scheduling Jane Bowles for a reading-personal appearance sometime after she had died. Oh well—only in America!

The Kerouac Conference, besides moving me in the direction of improved health, threw me into contact with what amounted to the celebrity world of the New Left (about a decade past its peak). I found myself requesting autographs from new heroes Abbie Hoffman and Timothy Leary and learning from Abbie that we had a mutual acquaintance from different contexts: the poet Jack

Stern—from my psychiatric context and from Abbie's political context (Strange how these worlds overlap!). At one point Abbie was humming, "Gerd Stern (aka Jack) is a nut . . ."

I would rise early at the Chautauqua Lodge in Boulder and wake everybody up with conversations from the porch about Mookie Wilson. Ted Berrigan (who died shortly thereafter) was my usual fellow conversationalist.

I roomed at Boulder with Ray Bremser, who smoked everything to a disastrous degree, and spent much of my time (especially in the early morning) with Jack Micheline—a charming maverick among the Beats, who saved me from the fate of becoming a mere Ginsberg sycophant.

All this dwelling on the Baghdad-like fascination of the present or near-present overlooks two other phases which gave me some early fame-notoriety (it seems in retrospect that *every* phase of my life cast me in some sort of limelight). First was the Brooklyn College dadaist potato salad throwing demonstration (before that a City College flirtation with the Cominform, successor, to those ignorant of the subject, of the Third International). Speaking of jumping out of the frying pan and into the fire, I have been always doing just this as one nutty phase leads straight into the next nutty phase and Carly (me) is always amazing somebody or other.

Just past the Fourth. Had Steve up yesterday to clean my room and to help give Jack (my uncle) a shower. Planning a big jaunt by Amtrak to Washington next week to see Aunt Bea and Lothar and Paula, my cousin. I haven't been in DC since 1977 when it was the Carter capital. I have found DC endlessly interesting. Perhaps the period that was most interesting for me was during the war, in an FDR administration, when my cousin Rudy was assistant counsel to the Truman War Investigating Committee. I stayed with Grace and Rudy then, hiked along the canal and in Rock Creek Park and down by the Jefferson Memorial, where I also chatted with fishermen fishing for "river cats" in the Potomac. They used balls of corn meal for bait.

Rudy got me passes to witness a session of Congress and I was thrilled to ride on the subway between the House and the Senate.

"Life doesn't come in neatly boxed manuscripts," said Lucien Carr to me one day in the eighties while we sat fishing in a rowboat off City Island. I had been complaining about the scroll manuscript of *On The Road* Jack Kerouac had brought to me when I was his editor back in the sainted fifties. Lucien should know. And now even the naive Mr. Solomon knows that life does not come neatly boxed either. In those days I wore button-down shirts and had all my teeth. Now I am not as glossy but have more in my head. I will not be a second Maxwell Perkins—but who cares? I came into this world as a kind of messenger, bawling out good tidings, and I shall leave as one, carrying a messenger service ID in my postmortem wallet.

In the summer of 1947 I could have stayed on in Paris. I was young enough, only 19, without important ties in the States, and I could have decided to hack out an existence as an expatriate. But the important factor was that I was hungry; I wasn't getting enough to eat in Paris. I had lost weight and I was shelling out money to my whore, Odette. Something had to be done. I couldn't live on jars of Bovril. I had to go back home for one reason—to eat. And I knew that, whatever else you may think of the USA, you could be sure to get enough to eat there (at least in those days). This may sound like a peculiar kind of patriotism to you, but those States on the map represented a heaping bowl of beef stew to me. I came back aboard the *Marine Jumper* (US Lines) and my heart, quite honestly, leaped with joy when I spotted the slices of white American bread on the supper table. As an expatriate, for the summer of 1947, I had been eating the coarse postwar French bread of those years (I still remember the baguettes). In spite of mental breakdowns and sometimes wacky underbelly living, I have never, in all those years since '47, gone hungry for very long in the USA. A peculiar kind of patriotism, having very little to do with Francis Scott Key—but every bit as genuine.

Of the men I work with one is named Winston and another Lyndon. Winston is about 50 years old, which indicates he was named after Churchill; the other is about 24, which indicates he was named after Johnson. There is a kind of magic in living through a period and then many years later encountering men named after the important statesmen of the earlier era. Which reminds me of Franklin, whom I worked with at Korvettes.

Something about Ollie North (I am watching the Irangate hearings now) reminds me of Kerouac. A kind of blunt apparent honesty. Which could also be suspect. Asked about beatness, Kerouac looked honestly at you and said, "Seeing the face of God." To me (and perhaps to me alone), North seems to make similar demands on everyday cynical credibility when he talks about fighting for democracy through the Contras. I think of Somoza and the Somoza officers among the Contras. Democracy?

The beatnik quality has fallen away from my life as the principals have died and/or been forgotten. I signed about twenty copies of "Howl" for bookdealer Roger Richards last week. That is about all that remains of years and a movement that once seemed exciting to me. Who can forget my early Gillespie records and my first brush with pot and illegality? Good boy become bad boy. Yes, for a short while it seemed exciting. Somehow though the early evaluations have crept back into my thinking. Pot I now reject primarily because of its adverse effect on my emphysemic lungs. This avoids the old issue of effect on the mind. As a matter of fact, I have deliberately shunned the mental issues entirely during this present phase of my life and think more of the physical health, spiritual, and political matters I have discussed. Not merely don't I want a rose-garden anymore, but over and beyond that I hope that all the aspects of mental patient life style are behind me—from the fisticuffs to the drug use to the sexual preoccupations to the time-wasting.

My good resolutions will probably hold up this time if only because there is no longer sufficient time or opportunity to break them—*and* the iron will that enabled to me to give up smoking (three and a half years so far since I gave up butts).

The war. A short time after siding with De Gaulle against Giraud, or preferring Tito to Mikhailovitch, I took to emulating Soviet marshals in my coiffure and facial expressions. I wore close-cropped hair and adopted a whole mental set which conformed with American identification with the Soviets during a brief and by now totally forgotten phase in American history. I don't condemn this fickleness of people but accept it as a fact of life. There was a whole set of expressions and attitudes that went with being a CPA-er during the forties. Besides the Soviet affectations, there was the exposure to old labor movement idiom—terms like "Jimmy Higgins work" which I had never heard outside the progressive movement. "Petty bourgeois" and "opportunist." "If you've got a lingo, you've got it made." All of which is evidence of the transience of history and the chronic and self-serving amnesia of the intellect. One may let oneself in for surprises by considering the past dead. You never know when it may crop up again in an incongruous context. Bits of paper, old documents, mortifying memories. Nothing is ever final, but always refurbishing, remoulding. (The CPA was the Communist Political Association, the form that the American CP took during the war—which seemed real and then an illusion.)

II

AN INTERVIEW WITH CARL SOLOMON

JOHN TYTELL: When did you first travel to Europe?

CARL SOLOMON: I joined the Merchant Marine in 1945, just before the war with Japan ended. I went to various places, France among them, and I jumped ship in 1947 in France. . . . I stayed there, went to Paris, and learned about Artaud, and Michaux, and Isou.

JT: Isn't it curious that so many writers like Kerouac and Ginsberg were joining the Merchant Marine?

CS: Well, there were movies in those days romanticizing it—*Action in the North Atlantic* with Humphrey Bogart—so that sort of thing was in the air then.

JT: Before going to sea you attended City College?

CS: I started there in 1943, when I was fifteen.

JT: When did you leave City College?

CS: Well, I kept on shipping out intermittently, going to school one term and to sea the next.

JT: So you were an early dropout?

CS: Yes, although I hadn't dropped out completely. I had neglected my studies really, and I got sort of low grades.

JT: Were there any teachers there that you still remember?

CS: Leffert, he was a specialist in Modern Literature—a very sharp, very classy sort of guy who seemed to love Gide.

JT: Was there anyone else?

CS: Then I had Abraham Edel in Philosophy who was very bright.

JT: Was CCNY a very active place politically?

CS: Yes. While I was there I joined the AYD (American Youth for Democracy). This was the Communist-front organization of that period when they were anti-Axis and for the war. The AYD group was known as the Tom Paine Club. The Communist Party went out of existence then, and they called it the CPA—Communist Political Association—during the Browder period, which is now regarded as a revisionist period. Browder felt there would be collaboration between capitalism and communism, and that the Party should go out of existence. So I joined the CPA which was part of the progressive movement and it was considered the left.

JT: Is this the origin of what is now known as Progressive Labor?

CS: No, no, no. That's Maoist and from the second wave of leftism in the late fifties or early sixties.

JT: Do you remember whether many students were similarly involved?

CS: Yeah. They had a very large membership. As a matter of fact, during those years the Communists dominated the CIO (Congress of Industrial Organizations), and they even elected two members to the New York City

Council in those years, Ben Davis and Cacchione in Brooklyn.

JT: Didn't you also attend Brooklyn College at one time?

CS: Well, I broke with my CP friends that I had made at CCNY, and I moved down to the Village and became interested in avant-garde art and existentialism with a circle of people disillusioned with the left, ex-liberals and progressives I should say. I began to read *The Partisan Review*, and a flock of other little magazines like *Horizon*. I went to Brooklyn College because I had a friend going there who said that it would be better for my literary interests than CCNY which was geared for engineers and science.

JT: In Mishaps, Perhaps, *you write that you witnessed an Artaud reading in Paris, 1947.*

CS: First of all I was looking for existentialists. So I went wandering around Saint-Germain-de-Pres and came to a gallery with a crowd standing outside. I can't recall the name of the street, but I read an account about it when I returned in *Partisan Review*, how Artaud had been screaming his "Damnation of the Flesh"—I've forgotten the rue (Was it rue Jacob?), but to me it's the rue Impasse or Satan. So I stood outside, and first a young man with black hair descended from upstairs, and he was trembling, and he read what I later found out was Artaud's "Ci-Git" preceded by the "Indian Culture"; then I remember another man in a turban screaming. He had been there before the young man. Originally, I had thought the young man was Artaud, but later I learned Artaud was an older man then—he was 51. I remember one line the young man read: "Papa, Maman et pédérast inné" and that tickled Kerouac in later years. The story I gave to him was that the reader was pointing at me but he was really pointing at the crowd.

JT: Did you have any further interest in Artaud?

CS: Oh yes. In 1948 I worked on a ship again since they hadn't ousted me for deserting and I went back to France. This time I got a couple of days off from my job as a dishwasher, and I made the long trip to Paris just for one day where I bought, in the same neighborhood, Artaud's book, *Van Gogh, The Man Suicided by Society.*

JT: I wanted to ask you about that. In Mishaps, Perhaps *you summarize Artaud's condemnation of all psychiatry, and his argument that those who are in turn condemned by psychiatrists are gifted with a superior lucidity and insight. It occurs to me that such notions are extremely prevalent in radical psychiatry in England and America today with people like R.D. Laing, David Cooper and Thomas Szasz.*

CS: Yes, today. Artaud began to be absorbed in certain areas later on. When I first read Artaud it was still something very esoteric. Later, when the theater of the absurd became prominent, his theatrical ideas at least came through. Anyway, I got *The Man Suicided by Society*, and then moved to West Fourth Street and attended Brooklyn College. At that time I was spending a lot of time in the 42nd Street Library where I found the lettrist magazine, *La Dictature Lettriste*, and I read through that. I was twenty years old at the time, and reading Artaud's letters. Then I cooked up a thing with Leni Grunes and Ronnie Gold—who is now one of the heads of the Gay Activists—and we staged a dadaist demonstration, and threw potato salad at Markfield.

JT: Wallace Markfield?

CS: Yes, he was lecturing on Mallarmé.

JT: Isn't there a line in "Howl" about that experience?

CS: Yes. At that time Ronnie and I were discussing the validity of suicide, and I read *Lafcadio's Adventures*, you know, the idea of the gratuitous crime, but I backed out of all this. I did steal a sandwich at Brooklyn College and showed it to the policeman, got sent to the psychologist, and then they sent me up to the Columbia Psychiatric Institute. I was in a very negative, nihilistic mood, things seemed so sick to me, and I wanted a lobotomy, or to be suicided. I thought I was a madman.

JT: Was this in any way a reaction to a dullness in the culture you felt at the time?

CS: Yeah, it was a reaction. Just before that my mother and I had moved to Parkchester, which I used to refer to as a Cubist colony because of the way it was arranged, cold, abstract, futuristic, regular houses which are now very common, but that was the first of the large projects. My old neighborhood, Prospect Avenue in the South Bronx, had been an ordinary sort of Jewish neighborhood with brownstones.

JT: Was this the Amalgamated project?

CS: No, Metropolitan Life Insurance Company, and in the beginning they didn't let Negroes in, you know, it was a place where everybody seemed to be a stereotype. And my rebellion against that led to the avant-garde involvement which led to the insulin shock treatment up at Columbia Psychiatric.

JT: Isn't that where you met Allen Ginsberg in a Dostoevskian encounter with you introducing yourself as Kirilov, and Allen introducing himself as Myshkin?

CS: Yes, I met Allen after coming down from the insulin ward, just emerging from a coma; comas, no less, to come out of reading and ideas! The story is in my

"Afterthoughts of a Shock Patient." When I came out of the hospital, supposedly cured, Allen introduced me to Neal Cassady and that bunch, and Landesman.

JT: Had you appeared in Neurotica *before?*

CS: No. Before that I wasn't really interested in *Neurotica*, although I had seen it around.

JT: What was Landesman like?

CS: He had an art gallery in St. Louis, a patron of the arts, and as Jack Kerouac characterized him he was a playboy.

JT: John Clellon Holmes has an interesting description of him in Nothing More to Declare.

CS: They were close friends.

JT: You met Allen in '49? He had been placed there because of the ride and Little Jack Melody. How many months were you together at that time?

CS: Oh, a couple of months, and I got out before he did.

JT: Did you have freedom to meet?

CS: We used to meet on the ward, and write, and read things to one another. I introduced him to works of Artaud and Genet; he read Yeats to me, Melville, and spoke of his friends, Kerouac and Burroughs. But he was highly critical of me. He thought my ideas at that time would lead me to a worse insanity, and perhaps under his suggestion that's what ultimately happened when I went to Pilgrim State.

JT: Well, that is a kind of negative influence.

CS: I suppose it was.

JT: In More Mishaps, *you write that Allen was taking notes on your adventures while at Columbia Psychiatric, and some of those notes appeared in a different form in "Howl."*

CS: He sat there, and I used to come out with very surrealistic aphorisms which he would transcribe.

JT: Can you remember some instances in your life that are reflected, however prismatically, in "Howl?"

CS: The remark about the pubic beards was mine, and the harlequin talk of suicide.

JT: In your books, I thought I detected a sign of hostility as well as admiration towards Ginsberg and his literary friends.

CS: I was angry because of my second sickness. I thought that they had all rejected me because I was madder than they were. I thought that they were neurotics and I was a psychotic, an outsider.

JT: In your books you always tease your readers with differences you had with Ginsberg, such as the way you saw Whitman.

CS: We were continually fighting. I saw Whitman as a political revolutionary, and Allen saw him as a sexual revolutionary. When I first met Allen I called him a "dopey daffodil" because he symbolized to me what poetry was then, referring to Wordsworth, I guess, the idea of poets as sensitive souls rather than Artaud's conception of the poet as brute. But Allen turned out not to be a dopey daffodil at all, but that's the way he looked then, a neat haircut and horn rim glasses. He seemed to me to be like the conventional English major who couldn't stand up to me at all. I thought I was much greater than these types, much more unconventional. I identified with the Beat Generation in much the same way as Artaud himself identified with the Surrealists: he felt that they were his ultimate enemy.

JT: You mean as a possible close source of betrayal because they couldn't really live up to his ideals?

CS: Yeah. Like when I escaped from Pilgrim State Hospital once I went over to Allen's brother's house, and while he talked to me, his wife called the hospital.

JT: How did you escape?

CS: I just walked off.

JT: What kind of treatment did you receive at Psychiatric Institute? Was it group therapy or individual analysis?

CS: Individual; they had group therapy at Pilgrim State.

JT: What kind of analyst did you have at Columbia Psychiatric—what school was he from?

CS: She—Washington School—Harry Stack Sullivan.

JT: What about Allen's analyst?

CS: I think he was Freudian. We had many fights about our analysts and their virtues. That happens in all hospitals, by the way. There was a situation out at Pilgrim State where the gentile patients wanted Jungian analysts, and the Jewish patients wanted Freudians.

JT: In Mishaps, Perhaps *you state that you had been conditioned in illness by classical surrealism.*

CS: I meant Artaud's void. Also ideas like the derangement of the senses, and things that Ronnie Gold and I used to do. We used to hang out in gay bars then, Mary's and Main Street which were both on Eighth Street in the Village, hubs of activity then. They were crowded outside and inside, a real super-decadent atmosphere. Ned Rorem used to go there, he was always at the bar. Ronnie Gold and I used to eat benzedrine. To me decadence meant absinthe, or green drinks like pernod, or creme de menthe. My idea of decadence was something that made Jack Kerouac write to me when I was at Pilgrim State: "Lautreamont, cafe noir, sans sucre." I never actually became a junkie or anything like that, and I was probably really afraid of more serious drugs, so I sort of dabbled in safe affectations. Stanley Gould says that I talked my way into all these hospitals, that I gave them the impression of being sick without really being sick.

JT: Do you think you were helped by being in those hospitals?

CS: It was bad as far as my record goes.

JT: I don't mean that, but your general attitudes to life and yourself?

CS: Oh sure. At Pilgrim State, for instance, by urging wholesome things on me, a tame life, the attendant used to treat me like a soldier and say to me "front and center." The psychologists tried to steer me away from the Beat Generation.

JT: Did you learn the lesson of psychiatry as being an adjustment, in fact an acceptance of exactly what you were re-

belling against? I would equate that with aging, with abandoning or forgetting youth.

CS: Well, I find myself in that position now.

JT: In Mishaps, Perhaps, *you claimed that your friends in 1949 made you assume the role of a lunatic saint. Who did you mean specifically?*

CS: Oh, Leni and that bunch, like Bob Reisner who was in my class at Brooklyn College, he wrote a book on graffiti. They thought that kind of thing was great. Reisner and I used to do many funny things, like I once pretended to be W.H. Auden at some exhibition, and there I was signing Auden's name.

JT: Somewhere in Mishaps, Perhaps *you mention that you were betrayed by Wilhelm Reich. I couldn't understand what you meant by that.*

CS: I have this anger at anybody who has done anything against me or criticized me in any way. So now up in the Bronx I'm just the poor innocent who has returned completely healthy after being driven mad by the captious criticism of all the intellectuals in the Village with their Reich and all the rest of it. And also I go back to the days when I was in high school at James Monroe, where I was into Whitman who seemed to me to be the greatest poet, and all these others were into more sophisticated things like Eliot—but that wasn't so bad—the worst was that some of them were into Reich. These same people were criticizing me as being overly naive about sexual matters, but to me they were trying to shock me, while generally mocking me.

JT: How did Junky, *Burroughs' first novel, get to you?*

CS: My uncle, A.A. Wyn, was the publisher of Ace Books. He gave me a job, and I was trying to make a big impression, and Allen thought it was a great idea to bring out these writers, and if we could make Genet and these others well known to the American public we would be accomplishing something. I don't see what we've accomplished, but we were trying to do that anyway, to change the consciousness. It was largely an educational mission.

JT: And Wyn was interested in this project?

CS: Yes. I don't think he was primarily interested in the commercial end, I think he saw their possibilities as writers.

JT: Did Allen give you the manuscript of Junky?

CS: We got it chapter by chapter from Burroughs in Mexico City. He would send them to Allen who brought them to me at Ace.

JT: That's about Burroughs' earliest writing, although I've read in the correspondence up at Columbia University that he and Kerouac collaborated on a detective book right after World War II.

CS: He sent me another book, *Queer.*

JT: Why didn't that get published?

CS: My uncle and I didn't feel it was up to *Junky.* That's never been published, but it probably should have been, especially for anybody interested in Burroughs' work. I once made him very angry because when he sent up *Queer,* I suggested that we should change the title to *Fag,* and Burroughs wrote back to Allen saying that he would cut my balls off because he made a distinction between the words, a fag being someone effeminate and a queer is a masculine type of homosexual.

JT: I have a hunch that parts of Queer *may have found a way into* Naked Lunch. *Did you have any correspondence with Burroughs in later years?*

CS: Yes, in Pilgrim State. He once sent me a cryptic note saying I should become a waiter. I didn't know whether he meant that I should wait until I was cured, or whether I should work in restaurants.

JT: He was opposed to psychoanalysis. He profoundly distrusts it.

CS: He probably did.

JT: In your preface to Junky *you call Burroughs "a curious adventurer."*

CS: Because of things like his trip to the Amazon.

JT: As well as mental trips inside the mind. By the way, have you read his more recent work, The Wild Boys, *for instance?*

CS: I glanced at *The Exterminator*; I've been selling it. I'm a little wary of Burroughs now because he's into a kind of general espousal of youth revolt, and it's necessary for me in my present state to keep a very straight, pro-social, even patriotic outlook. During the Vietnam thing I participated in no protests; I voted for Procaccino, and I was on the verge of voting for Nixon, but I ended up voting for McGovern. But at the same time I'm doing crazy things like reading Marx.

JT: In Mishaps, 'Perhaps *you discuss—not in connection with Burroughs but with surrealism—the impulse to make the ugly beautiful which is just the approach I am taking in my own attempts to describe Burroughs' fiction. You also deal with diabolism.*

CS: All this is secondary, later than "The Report from the Asylum" which I still consider the clearest statement of my ideas—after that I was just trying to relate to my legend. That's where the diabolist stuff occurs.

JT: Then you have no chronology in your book because the "Report" is near the end?

CS: Yeah, there aren't any dates. At the time I wrote "Report from the Asylum" I was very careful, and I used to edit closely, but I reached a phase where the whole thing got out of my control, sometimes agreeing to things I disliked out of weariness or confusion. Of course legally, I lost my rights in 1956 when I was committed to Pilgrim State.

JT: Getting back to your work as an editor at Ace, I understand that you were also at one time considering publishing Kerouac?

CS: We had paid him an advance of $500, and I had visions of myself as being his Maxwell Perkins and him being my Wolfe because his first novel resembled Wolfe.

JT: I read a letter you wrote to Kerouac at Columbia University Special Collections in which you said that the Wolfean aspect of The Town and the City *was a charade that bespoke a repressed surrealism and a repressed homosexuality.*

CS: I must have been very erudite in those days.

JT: What happened with the contract because Kerouac never published with Ace Books?

CS: Well, we rejected *On the Road*—he sent us this long scroll. My uncle said it looked like he took it from his trunk.

JT: The teletype roll. Did he get that from Lucien Carr at United Press?

CS: I don't know where he got it, but we were used to these neat manuscripts, and I thought, "Gee, I can't read this."

JT: You didn't accept it as a surrealist antic, then?

CS: Because at that time I probably wasn't into that. I went through many phases while I was an editor: a Buddhist phase, then I read this book, *Philosophy of a Lunatic*, ultimately.

JT: Who wrote that?

CS: John Custance. Nobody has ever heard of the book but me. I bought it in the Gotham Book Mart while working for Ace Books. To me it seemed the ultimate mind-blowing thing, going beyond Zen which was a great step toward the elimination of myself. It was an existentialist version of Armageddon, the forces of God against the forces of the devil.

JT: What was Kerouac's attitude to publishers in general?

CS: Bad! He thought of them as skinflints, and he used the term "Broadway Sams"—he meant Jewish liberal intellectuals. He was snide about anybody who worked in offices.

JT: Was there any problem with getting Kerouac to make revisions?

CS: Yes. He got very angry when I wrote him suggestions.

JT: Did Kerouac send you anything after On the Road?

CS: Then I flipped and was sent to Pilgrim State. But the house continued to deal with him, and they accepted things, and then later reversed themselves.

JT: Did Kerouac try to interest you in publishing Cassady?

CS: He had mentioned that Neal Cassady wrote, but he wasn't trying to get us to accept anything. That later became *The First Third.*

JT: Did you ever meet Neal Cassady?

CS: Oh yeah. When I came out of Columbia Psychiatric Allen wanted me to throw a New Year's party. So I got a cold water flat on 17th Street and threw a party at which Neal Cassady was one of the star performers. He played one of those sweet potato things that make music, you know, and we were wearing those funny noses with the bebop eyeglasses.

JT: I've heard that Cassady had magnetic sexual appeal.

CS: Not to me.

JT: What was his appeal, then?

CS: He was always bouncing around—sort of kinetic energy more than anything else.

JT: What about his speech? His rambling monologues?

CS: He did one funny routine at the New Year's party, an Amos and Andy routine.

JT: He was influenced by radio?

CS: He knew a lot about popular culture. He was very American where a lot of us were rather frenchified.

JT: What kind of jobs have you worked in your life? In Mishaps, Perhaps *you have this anecdote about selling ice cream in front of the United Nations.*

CS: That was after "Howl" had just come out, and I was considered to have gone mad again. I was working for Eskimo Ace. I've worked on ships as a messman, in the steward's department, as an editor, with books in bookstores, when I was sixteen on a farm in Smyrna, New York, where I shoveled manure and worked a horse-drawn plow trying to make even furrows, and earlier, when I was fourteen I bundled the Sunday *Times*. I also worked for Nugent National Stores in the garment district, and delivered *Womens' Wear Daily*. When I met Allen we all worked in market research. I was married then, and my wife and I coded for NORC. John Holmes also worked there.

JT: Let's talk about your own writing. One of the qualities I love in it is your humor which is so often a function of epigram, puns and word play, like calling Poe's "The Raven" "the ravin." Or saying that if you lose contact with the zeitgeist, never fear, you may reach the poltergeist.

CS: The use of puns is not entirely natural to me. That was the Michaux influence.

JT: Can you find ways to sustain that humor in your own life?

CS: I've tried, but it's dropped off. Now my jokes are very bad. I've exhausted my humor, and can't work my brain to that extent because I have to be responsible for my own functioning.

JT: Do you feel that you were part of a movement?

CS: As a matter of fact, I hadn't felt that. I had just been through with a movement, and I had an aversion to movements—after all I had just finished with the Communists. I was living on 113th Street, and I knew this guy Don Cook, and he first mentioned the idea of a movement in reference to the Beats, and I was shocked—here I was trapped by something I had been trying to get away from!

November 7, 1973

III
CARL'S STORY

CHAPTER ONE

I was born in a red house or at least there I first became aware of myself as a being on this planet with a future destiny ahead. My father was named Moe, my mother Anne.

I lit my first cigarette at twenty-one since I had now become of age to smoke.

At fifteen I had a certain interest in the arts.

My favorite author was Saroyan.

At Prospect Avenue my greatest interests were baseball and fishing.

Moe and I were at the Polo Grounds or at Yankee Stadium regularly.

I remember all the great Yankee teams of the thirties.

I liked the Cincinnati team of '39—Derringer and Walters etc.

Gehrig was my favorite player.

WAR TOYS

Tomorrow will be the 50th anniversary of uncle Alan's death. I remember him primarily for his criticism of my parents for buying me war toys. I was a little too blood-thirsty for his taste. The toys he was most critical of were a conglomeration of soldiers, Indians, knights, mortars, forts etc. which figured largely in solitary fantasies I loved to engage in during my leisure hours.

MY FATHER

He was very patriotic, and made me salute the flag every time one passed by. He wanted me to be "an officer and a gentleman." He told stories of World War I, and had a very low opinion of President Wilson. He recounted how the American troops had been addressed by Gabriele D'Annunzio and how the Italian Fascist poet had derided Wilson. As I think back, I recall how his sympathies had been pretty generally on the extreme right. My left-wing period of the forties, after he died in '39, must have been a sharp and bitter reaction to his teachings. I am not sure whether his teachings or the teachings of others have been more lasting in their effect on me. It has certainly given me a breadth of political understanding that enables me to see both points of view and to understand most sub-divisions of thought even if it has not given me a philosophy to live by at all times.

THE SONG OF ROLAND

This was in the days before karate. When I heard only vague rumblings of Marx and Freud in living room family discussions competing with pinochle games. Long before the existentialists were even heard of by ordinary people. Before bebop and rock 'n' roll. I was a kid. My father moulded my first reading habits and this tended toward the study of chivalry and medieval romance. The friendship of Roland and Oliver was a part of this and I often longed for such a friendship. Before I read Legman or Leslie Fiedler. Anyway, I never did make such a friendship. Not in those years and not later. Women always intervened and they would always somehow set the males against one another. I did have a sword. The sword was the most important part of my get-up. Once, my father and I went into the backyard to practice duelling. The swords were fashioned from heavy pieces of wood. I wounded him on the finger accidentally, causing a small blood clot to appear. I felt terrible about it; I cried.

Chivalry disappeared from my thoughts almost from the day he died, when I was eleven. Other elements immediately intervened. When he died, naturally, everyone I knew felt sorry for me, so stricken was I by the loss of my best, albeit older pal. This is the way it has been ever since. "Don't waste time thinking about *Song of Roland*. Get with it. Get with it. Find other interests. Get with it." But the connection to other interests has never been fully made. I have, since eleven, flitted from individual to individual, hoping they would share with me a morsel of their interests.

Yet I have always appeared bereft and this was why. If I appeared Beat, this and not gratuitous despair was the reason for my "Beatness." A loss that nothing could ever replace. This was the reason for the Void. Perhaps it is the explanation for Dada. These poets missed their Dada. What other possible explanation?

RE QUIET LEFTY

The only true fictional character I have ever created I created when I was 14 in a high school creative writing class and I called him Quiet Lefty. I had him continually inhabiting the dumps in that deserted desolate area of the Bronx next to the East River. During the Depression years, this area was dotted with lean-tos hastily constructed and inhabited by hobos and all manner of fantastic characters. There were also old Italian men who kept goats there. School boys would go down there to dive nude off the pier that jutted into the river. One day, my friend and I went down there on a scientific mission—to capture paramecia for our general science class. We carried a jar and filled it with polluted water. It was in this area that I situated Quiet Lefty. And he was continually being nagged by a nasty, crotchety character known as The Green Man. Quiet Lefty chased him away one day throwing rocks at him and calling him "*a schmuck.*" I used this word in the original story, not knowing what it meant but having heard it used frequently and it created terrible consternation in the class, one of the fellows better schooled in profanity than I explaining to me that it referred to the male organ. The teacher, liberal in her views, gave me an "A" for the piece. This was my first though unwitting excursion into obscenity.

AVERSION TO SOME HORSES

Having been born in the crowded city, some years after the disappearance of the horseless carriage, I should like to describe in limited detail the role that the equine species has played in my life. At 16, I worked one summer on a dairy farm and did some plowing with a pair of horses. I feared them, though I didn't let on, and they did me no harm and were obedient enough. Around that time, I took a trip to Miami to satisfy my curiosity about that town. In the boarding house I stayed in was a group of sharp, stealthy-looking men who the landlady referred to as "the horsey people"—inveterate horseplayers. They seemed to take no notice of me at all and were continually buzzing about and using an argot which to me was completely incomprehensible. Some years later, while on a vacation from my publishing job and deep in the throes of an infatuation with Zen Buddhism, just before the onset of an imminent psychosis, I visited a dude ranch in the Catskills and again was completely ignored, not spoken to once in a whole weekend by a group of equally "horsey" people who had chosen riding as a way of life. However, I did recently enjoy watching the Derby on TV and imagine that more association with horses would make me like them better than I do.

As I write, another incident comes to mind—one in which I worked on a ship carrying horses as U.S. aid to Poland in 1946. These horses inspired considerable sympathy in me and when one died en route, I was so affected that I wrote a story about his death for a short story writing course I took shortly after I returned to NY. So you see, my feelings about horses and their effect upon man are mixed.

Nor have I ever used "horse."

JAZZ

As a boy, I was left completely cold by all forms of music other than patriotic airs and couldn't stand jazz until I began reading *The Partisan Review* in the late forties, and partook of the bebop-cum-Dostoyevski vogue. America, in general, I think, became more jazz conscious than it had ever been in the late forties with the origin of the progressive jazz movement and *"hip"* thought. In addition to squares, enemies included the *"moldy figs,"* admirers of the, by then, officially outmoded Dixieland style. It was this interest which put me in contact with the Ginsberg-Kerouac crowd of the early fifties.

MEMORY OF A HAMMOCK

I did most of my summertime reading in about '41 or '42 in a hammock that was strung out at a place where we spent the summer. One of the books I remember as having been most engrossing was *Drums Along The Mohawk* by Walter Edmonds. This type of book had great appeal to me in those years, in fact, anything about covered wagons or knights in armor or about Andrew Jackson and Jean Lafitte, the bayou pirate, had great appeal to me in those days and, I suspect, still might. I am going back to those years for memories and books and trying not to let everybody's present intrude on mine. Solitude, I think, makes readers and writers. It is underestimated today and I have certainly associated with enough people in the last 25 years to value solitude. Away from the *"in"* crowd and the *"out"* crowd and crowds in general.

INDIANS

My favorite tribe was the Iroquois. I collected arrowheads. Also liked the Wyandots. I'd wanted to tan my skin so as to resemble an Indian. Images of war; the French against the Indians, at school. Montcalm and Wolfe both

dying on the Plains of Abraham, outside Quebec. Took
a trip with the family to Quebec, in the thirties. I ran
around the Plains of Abraham while my father took pleasure in the historic meaning of the occasion. Images of
the Whiskey Rebellion that we saw in school. Not bad at
all. I liked the Green Mountain Boys and Mad Anthony
Wayne. Buffalo Bill Cody and Wild Bill Hickok, too. Like-
wise Jean Arthur and Calamity Jane. Those were definitely the good days. Of Freud, I knew only that Eugene
O'Neill was interested in his theories. Very literary household. Two uncles and an aunt, writers. Uncle well-known
as a playwright on Broadway. Same mess today. Still the
same old thing. Why does the name "Humperdinck" stand
out in my mind? Yes, now I remember. Humperdinck
was also a writer. Probably German or Austrian. Know
very little about Humperdinck, except that somebody
translated him and that somebody else made a dish out
of him. Long live Humperdinck.

AT THE MOMENT IT HAPPENED
THE OLD RIGHT

The most pressing issue of the day is the corruption
of youth and the far-reaching prevalence of masturbation—mutual and one-handed. Those damned brats
really bug me. They think they're so smart. They light
up a joint and lose all respect. Not a thing. To show what
I mean, they've just published a book where it is claimed
that Gary Cooper was a fag. Come on, Gary Cooper was
my favorite actor. At least I'm old enough to remember
the good old days. When I was a kid, I wasn't like the
kids these days. I always brushed my teeth. I didn't have

some damned degree in Marxist-Leninist phenomonology. I wasn't a Yippie and I never tried to be anything else. And then there was Foreign Affairs. We had a general assembly at my school, and there was always a *motion* on the issue, then a *for* and an *against*. I always took the side of the Chinese against the Japanese, and of Finland, which was a good country, because they had paid their World War I debt to the United States. On the Fourth of July we let off firecrackers, fireworks, everywhere. On election day, we had bonfires to burn the losers and honor the winners.

Carl W. Solomon
Diploma, James Monroe High School, 1943

P.S. Artaud said: "If I am told one more time that I'm crazy, I'm going to commit a crime." That sentence knocked me out when I was twenty. Everything else just followed naturally.

I WAS A COMMUNIST YOUTH

It was during the war. Red movements were flourishing everywhere. On the City College campus in 1944, when I began college, there were at least 500 supporters of the American Communist Party out of a student body of a couple of thousand. Such was the educational environment of the war generation. We were raised under these slogans: Win the war, destroy fascism. After the war full employment and the "century of the common man."

Fascism was the most hated philosophy of all time. Hitler and Mussolini and Tojo were seen as the most significant tyrants of history.

Moods have changed and time has brought about a difference in us all. After the war, America was to break with her wartime allies and they were to grapple on the battlefields of Korea. The great disillusion was to come.

But there I stood, 15 years old and full of the propaganda of the day.

My travels brought me to Europe and to the West Indies and I had a glimpse of the world that the war against fascism had created.

I cannot say that it was or is a world that was sympathetic to ideas of return to the old order or a world which wanted to preserve the free enterprise system.

What I saw in Cuba in 1945 was a preview of what was to come in the late fifties.

What I saw in Yugoslavia in 1945 was the Partisans, wearing red stars on their arms.

I saw much the same thing, to a lesser degree, in France, Italy, and Greece.

Only in America and from America came the slogan: Freedom. The slogan freedom meant white supremacy and the suppression of every movement for human hope on the face of the planet. So the cold war began.

The men, like Franco of Spain, whom we had been taught to hate, we were now told were our allies in a struggle against the "Eastern Bloc."

Men like Dimitrov of Bulgaria who had had the courage to defy fascism during the thirties, we were told now were our enemies, a group of cowardly tyrants.

Who knows what his opinions are amid such nonsense.

THE CAT SOVIET

During those bitter thirties, during the Spanish Civil War, I also had other relatives whose apparent sympathies lay with the other side. An aunt of mine, since deceased, owned a red alley cat which she had dubbed "Soviet." Every time the cat walked by, she would call out: "Here, Soviet, Here, Soviet."

MY HENRY WALLACE PERIOD

This occurred at full blast about 1943, and I was completely taken with Henry Wallace and the Century of the Common Man. I cannot describe it except to indicate that at that time I was typical of the stereotype of the Wallace supporter.

I still associate my Walt Whitman phase with this type of ultrademocratic thinking, rather than with anything *"gay,"* though Allen connects Whitman somehow with sexual rather than political revolution. There are undoubtedly both elements in Whitman, even a Nietzschean strain, in spite of his often being claimed by the communists.

CITY COLLEGE

Seems like several lifetimes ago. It actually was 1943 when I entered City College as a freshman, 15 years old, facial hairs just beginning to grow. Entered as something then known as a Bachelor of Science in Social Science. I remember the Dean, a short, rather puny, but sensitive man named Morton Gottschall. I remember filtering into the school with some of my high school chums and how we tried to continue our adolescent friendships as we went into different classes peopled largely with students from other high schools. I remember buying gym clothes and sneakers and a combination lock. I was thrilled at the expansive gym with its polished wooden floor and equally by the swimming pool with its aquamarine water and its smell of chlorine. When we went into the cafeteria, we, from our high school group, tried to separate ourselves from the confusing mass of other students by isolating ourselves in a small part of the cafeteria known as The Alcove.

While I was slowly growing up in this fashion, in the real outer world, World War II was going on. The Russians at that time, led by our then beloved "Uncle" Joe Stalin (so referred to at that time in most of the New York press) were beginning to slow the German advance in the vicinity of Stalingrad and to chew up important parts of Hitler's heretofore invincible army. Caught up in the spirit of the time, I simultaneously became a member of the Reserve Officer's Training Corps of the U.S. Army and a member of the City College chapter of the Communist front youth organization, the American Youth For Democracy (the Tom Paine Club).

In the ROTC (a military science course officially) I wore a uniform, khaki with blue lapels, drilled in the drill hall, studied azimuth and similar subjects with a dapper young army officer named Lieutenant Yott, and learned to fire an M-1 rifle. The student leader of the ROTC around that time was a young black man who also was a member of the AYD. I knew who was and who was not a member of the organization because I was its membership secretary and handled all the applications for membership. I am not sure at this point in time just when the House Plan Sportin' Life phase ended and the radical political life began. They seem to converge in my memory. I remember becoming co-bookmaker of a basketball pool in conjunction with one of my House Plan companions during the then-unblemished period of CCNY's basketball ascendancy. I attended doubleheaders at the old Garden and was thrilled by the bouncy, tenacious magnificence of our team which then starred "Red" Holtzman, Sonny Hertzberg, Irwin Dambrot, and others, under the brilliant leadership of Nat Holman. Basketball superiority and academic superiority were then emblazoned on our individual banners and we looked upon Ivy League collegiate royalty rather defiantly. We were, after all, a tuition-free college.

Academically, an unusual thing was happening to me. I was becoming less interested in grades as such and was becoming seriously interested in certain subjects to the exclusion of others, becoming very seriously "turned on" by things like philosophy, English, and music. This intellectual ferment was proceeding hand-in-hand with a growing political interest and activity which was now consuming most of my time and separating me—as it turned out forever—from high school friends and interests. I began attending meetings and lectures and parties and musicales and countless other activities connected with the AYD. In the college cafeteria, I moved out of The Alcove, and over to the political tables where the AYD members sat. Guitars proliferated there. Seating areas could now be broken down politically. AYDers here, World Federalists there, Socialists in another place, Newman Club people in still another.

Outside, still, the war was going on, D-day had already occurred and one of my high school friends was reported killed in France. I was nearing the age when I would be eligible for one of the services and, as soon as I turned 17, I joined the one which was open to me then—which also happened to be in line with my interests—the U.S. Maritime Service. I left school, after having amassed an unimpressive academic record in the prior two years, and went into the Maritime Service. However, I had not dropped out. I was actually on a leave of absence. I received my maritime training at Sheepshead

Bay and sailed as a messman, galleyman, or bedroom steward to all ports of the Atlantic and Mediterranean world: Cuba, Italy, Poland, North Africa, Greece, Crete, France, Curacao, the Azores. Every so often, I would return to school for a term or two, retiring my National Maritime Union book for the interim—leading a split life as a seaman and as a student. When I went back to school, I would plunge into Theodore Goodman's short story course (where Joyce's "Dubliners" was the prime exemplary text) and write rambling accounts of my maritime adventures. Further, my interest in philosophy was soaring at this time and I found great stimulation in both Abraham Edel's philosophy course and Henry Leffert's English course. I was becoming interested in existentialism and probably in whatever other esoteric "ism" I could find a book about. I became a compulsive reader.

There was one other teacher at City whose course proved extremely valuable to me in my subsequent studies. That was Sol Liptzin, whose course in German literature awakened my interest in the German Romantic movement and finally in expressionism, a movement the nuances of which have become of increasing relevance to me in surveying the grotesqueries and ironies of contemporary life.

Meanwhile, the post-World War II world was beginning to take shape. The veterans were returning. Everywhere on the campus, one saw older fellows wearing "ruptured ducks" (the veterans' insignia of that war). Marriages and career shaping were now the important things, replacing the purer intellectual interests.

I hied myself over to Paris (I was now 19) and began investigating the worlds of jazz, existentialism, postwar Marxism, surrealism, subculture and psychiatry. When I came back from Paris, I was deeply into Rimbaud, symbolism and related subjects and had no interest anymore in what City College had to offer me. I was anything but "down-to-earth." In fact, very much the reverse. I was bored with the plodding rationalism of the CCNY students who seemed then to me to be interested in science and engineering and not at all in my by now eccentric, even "otherworldly," concerns. I was becoming "hip," avant-garde, and bohemian all in one and sought a farther-out scene for my new efflorescence.

I sought it by transferring, very suddenly, to Brooklyn College without ever graduating from CCNY. Records of courses completed, of things actually learned, chronology itself was becoming increasingly confused with all these ramblings and changes. Very, very often I seemed on the brink of losing my reason. My life was becoming a surrealist adventure, or so it seemed to me, rather than being the life of a normal New Yorker. I sought help through psychotherapy, through religion, through drug bits, through work stints, through marriage, through taking up dancing, through abstinence, through indulgence, through dieting, etc., etc., etc. So gradually our Bachelor of Science in Social Science of 1943 became a rather perplexed adult who struggled along decade after decade occasionally finding an outlet in writing, moving from job to job, from therapy to therapy, falling in love, falling out of love. City College friends would turn up from time to time, say "Hello" and move on. The period of study at City itself had a lasting influence however and my reading through the subsequent years on into the present was directly connected to things I had read or heard about at City.

One thing I would like to consider is whether all of this college exposure has been a good thing or a bad thing. It has been bad in so far as it has cut me off from many people who, having never had such exposure themselves, resent it in others. The intellectual or egghead label has been fixed on me very often in business life and in almost every other area of contemporary life I have ventured into. This has more often than not been to my apparent detriment. What hatred some men have for what they call "intellectuals!" You're never quite normal, never quite what you are supposed to be. There seems to be an eternal

conflict between the needs of standard operating procedure (which most men prefer to comply with unprotest-
ingly) and the mind of one who is a questioner. The man
who has been to college seems to be forever making waves,
forever rankling whoever bears unchallenged authority.
How often I have been told that "too much reading" can
make one "mentally ill." Yet, I have continued to be such
a gadfly and am still here. I suspect the anti-intellectual
of really having a "sour grapes" motivation behind his
disparaging remarks. In spite of never having finished
my college career, I am still often jokingly called "Doctor"
or "Professor" or being told I talk like an English teacher.

At City College one could drop in quite casually on
a discussion of Marx and Engels, or Trotsky or Freud or
Gide and not think that one had been exposed to the
most treasonable, scandalous, or sacrilegious subject matter in the world. Here was a genuinely literate and en-
lightened campus.

THE CITY OF ELECTRIC NIGHT

It wasn't so long ago, I was sitting in that English
class, and a note, passed down the long row of students,
was handed to me. That note! "Carl Solomon, your arms
are so soft." It was written to me by a young poetess. Yes,
I had soft arms in those days, and I was someone important in the Theatre Arts Club. I had created the position of "coordinator" for myself, following the example
of Leon Henderson, the OPA coordinator.

We gave a party, my friends and I, and we tried to
get everyone drunk on Cuba Libres, to free their inhi-
bitions. And we invited girls (!).

Leon Henderson and Sidney Hillman and girls (!).

(Hang on a second. I have to get dressed for work. I'll add more another day, when I have time to flirt with these memories.)

And pygmies shooting poisoned darts with their peashooters.

Plane geometry was a fascinating subject, and so was military science, but the first time I ever heard of Dada, it was from an English professor who gave Baudelaire as an example, because he had dyed his hair green.

The precise circumstances of my Dadaist initiatives during my university days, were that two of my casual acquaintances and I disrupted a lecture on "Mallarmé and Alienation." The plan we had devised: distribute very green peas among the listeners, wave a flag that was inscribed "Ausable Chasm," while, among other verbal taunts, I shouted, "The alien nation of Mallarmé was France," throwing a handful of potato salad in the lecturer's face.

THE CLASS OF '48

It was a bizarre group. Decadent in many ways, I thought. They seemed to feel that the war was over and that they would never be faced with any major challenges again. They are still with me. I meet them here and there, in the New School, in a mental hospital, on 42nd Street, in a bar. They were called then "The Silent Generation," later on "The Beat Generation." They were the precursors of the rock 'n' roll youngsters, but somehow neither sane enough nor mad enough, too young to have been in the war and too old to be Cold War products, a between-wars group.

Will any new influences ever jar them and me from their perpetual rut? From the boring indifference and insufficiently bleak pessimism that has been their heritage. I doubt whether anything ever will. Endless experimentation with the senses, endless metaphysical rambling. I am back in the Bronx, among the molding influences. On the subway twice a week, I pass and can see the high school I graduated from, James Monroe, and am recalled to the early heroic, pre-decadent days of my generation. When we were busy with scrap drives, orienting ourselves toward being public-minded citizens rather than hopped-up, disoriented nuts. The reaction was a hatred of regimentation, and when the reaction set in it was bitter and fatal to some. Perhaps, now that the fifties are forgotten, another reaction will set in, in the interests of self-preservation and order. The nihilistic period is past. The time for sincere creativity, I think is here.

PARTIZANI

1945. Youthful adventure story. Ship I was working on moored at Trieste. I wanted to see the Yugoslavs. Tito then was something that might be characterized as the Castro of that period. So I worked my way up and down the hills and vales of Trieste and out into the suburbs. Walked very fast, not being a smoker yet (at 17) and a much stronger walker than now. Long strides. Mountains ahead. The Dinaric Alps. Very thrilled at the thought of walking through any kind of Alps—especially Dinaric Alps which had a much more esoteric ring than mere majestic Swiss Alps. Also thrilled at the idea of being in on history in the making—the Yugoslavs had been threatening to move in on Trieste. Out into the hills, walking like an unstoppable express. Suddenly, out of the bushes, came the Partisans, about 14 years old and carrying sub-machine-guns. Followed in docile manner. They took me to some little shack and made me wait. Then put me in a cart drawn by I forget what type of animal. And so off through the mountains. At length deposited me in internment camp called Divacha. Talked to Displaced Persons there. I remember one Czech with whom I discussed Czechoslovakia. He talked much about "Ruda Slansky" and, if I recall right, thought him a bad man. Slansky later became better known in the West when he was executed in a purge. So chatted and ate the cereal and black bread they gave us and slept in wooden boxes like elongated orange crates arranged in tiers three high. My feet protruded and it was quite uncomfortable. I was interviewed and, in spite of their early suspicions that I was a German, they accepted my story that I was a humble messman from a ship moored at Trieste. They finally sent me back by train and, when I got back on the ship, the captain said, "Well, Wandering Willy, we'd almost thought you were lying dead in some alleyway in Trieste." The end, and still remembered when I unload my reminiscences of Service-type experience—not having been on Guadalcanal. This satisfies my claim to normalcy nowadays.

THE STORY OF THE SECOND STEWARD

This incident occurred in 1945 during a voyage of the Liberty ship, *John C. Breckinridge*, from New York to Trieste, a free city at the head of the Adriatic Sea then in dispute between Italy and Yugoslavia. I was working on the ship as a crew messman. I was wearing a ring made of a yellowish metal with an inscription, the Masonic inscription with the letter "G" on it. The Second Steward who had charge of the messmen was a Frenchman of about 50. I was then 17. The ring had been given to me by my mother, a widow who was at that time going out with a retired sea captain who had given the ring to her. About the third day out at sea, the Second Steward summoned me at the end of a meal and made a very serious face as he instructed me to remove the ring from my finger immediately because he had given me the Masonic high sign and I had not reciprocated, hence was ineligible to wear the ring. I immediately obeyed and the incident ended there but I had been left with a lifelong aversion to secret orders, cabals and hierarchies and all their mysterious folderol. This aversion has not served me well since most people seem to be members of some cabal or other, the rules of which I seem to be perpetually transgressing against.

A TASTE FOR NOUGAT

A kind of immature romantic at that time, full of flowery dreams of Paris—having just read to completion Romain Rolland's novel *Jean Christophe*—I deserted, very precipitously and foolishly, I later decided, the American Liberty ship *Alexander Ramsey*, in the port of La Pallice in Brittany (during May of 1947) and made my way to La Rochelle (the provincial capital). There my first move was to get a haircut.

Then, on to Paris, settled in Montparnasse, read *Tropic of Cancer*, and hired a French lady to teach me the language.

It was not long before I had developed a taste for nougat and haricots verts, attended a lecture on Kafka by Jean-Paul Sartre at the Salle Gaveau, seen the *Mona Lisa*, made friends at the Cité Université who had turned me on to Prévert and Michaux, begun an amatory relationship with a lady in Montmartre, witnessed an Artaud reading on the rue Jacob, attended a CP rally at the Vel d'Hiv, [Velodrome d'Hiver, Winter Garden, Paris assembly place for sports and political meets] and discovered Isou and *lettrisme*.

Six weeks and it was all over (the Paris *séjour*) and I came back to the States. Lettrism had already awakened an interest in me and I was especially interested in the new poets of my generation of whom Isou and his followers seemed to be very significant ones. The whole tendency toward the nonverbal as I witnessed its reflection even in such American phenomena as the scat singing of Jackie Cain and Ray Kraal [Singers who performed at Birdland, New York bebop mecca]. I sat in the 42nd Street library in those years reading the latest issues of *La Nouvelle Revue Française*. I remember a special issue devoted to "Young Men of Twenty" in the year 1948.

My protest against the verbal, the rational and the acceptable took the form of disruption of a critical discussion of Mallarmé and other neo-dada clowning, which resulted in my incarceration in a psychiatric hospital in Manhattan. Where I encountered Allen Ginsberg, a fellow patient who was intrigued by my collection of Paris-acquired books. Among the Artaud, Genet, Michaux, Miller, and Lautréamont was Isou's *Nouvelle Poésie et une Nouvelle Musique*. We discussed all of these things by way of laying the groundwork for Allen's eventual publication of "Howl" in 1956.

After treatment at PI, I was readmitted to Brooklyn College, dropped out after subsequent marriage and job offer in book publishing.

After release from Pilgrim State (post-"Howl") I took a battery of aptitude tests administered by the NY State Department of Vocational Rehabilitation which indicated an IQ slightly above average and aptitude in literature, sales and social service; deficiencies in mechanical, scientific and mathematical areas; I wasn't trying very hard.

I took courses in American literature at the New

School. NYU has been trying to get me back into academic work offering credit for life experience. However I still prefer to work.

BACKGROUND TO "HOWL": MEMOIRS OF THE WAUGH YEARS

It was Franklin Roosevelt who declared that he hated Evelyn Waugh. At the time he also stated that his wife Eleanor hated Waugh. I, on the contrary, loved Waugh. I remember reading three of his books consecutively immediately before concocting a unique suicide scheme: to be suicided by society à la Van Gogh. I picked up a peanut butter sandwich without paying for it in the Brooklyn College cafeteria, hoping to be fired upon and executed summarily by the huge cop on duty. At this time I was also influenced by the famous gratuitous crime in Andre Gide's *Les Caves Du Vatican*. What happened was no execution but an introduction to the head nurse at Manhattan's Psychiatric Institute where, history moving in strange ways, I met for the first time my fellow beatnik-to-be, Allen Ginsberg. I gave Allen an apocryphal history of my adventures and pseudo-intellectual deeds of daring. He meticulously took notes of everything I said (I thought at the time that he suffered from "the writer's disease," imagined that he was a great writer). Later, when I decided to give up the flesh and become a professional lunatic-saint, he published all of this data, compounded partly of truth, but for the most raving self-justification, crypto-bohemian boasting à la Rimbaud, and esoteric aphorisms plagiarized from Kierkegaard and others—in the form of "Howl." Thus he enshrined falsehood as truth and raving as common sense for future generations to ponder over and be misled. Lee Harvey Oswald had his Mark Lane—I had none. And needed none, such a man of action have I proven myself when confronted with the lies and false analyzing of my own generation—that glamorized assortment of nincompoops. I have wormed my way out of an infinite variety of asylums and proven that I am a good, honorable, Manitou-fearing, solid citizen—a sensitive humanist and litterateur. This in spite of the general pederasty to which I was exposed as a tender child. In spite of the influence of wizened academics who first led me astray by exposing me to seducers of youth like Gide, etc.

MEETING JULIAN BECK DURING THE PAPACY OF JOHN THE TWENTY-THIRD

Einstein said that time curved and it has always been difficult for me to keep an accurate chronology. Further, I read all of *La Recherche du Temps Perdu* at one point in the seventies and thought much about the Bergsonian difference between chronological time and psychological time. Fuck it anyway. Must have been about 1959 when I approached Mr. Boyle with some request or other and he, annoyed, said angrily, "Solomon, go back to the Bronx!"

I took it quite literally and sped out onto the grounds and beyond them out onto the Sunrise Highway in Long Island and walking very fast both walked and hitch-hiked toward NYC. I had no money at all and when I got hungry en route I spotted an empty coke bottle and turned it in to a grocery on the highway for some change which I rapidly converted into two Tootsie Rolls. I ate the Tootsie Rolls and sped onward toward the Apple.

Night fell, though, and I looked for a comfy, safe place to nap and found it in one of the many cemeteries that abut onto the Sunrise Highway. Came morning, I moved on.

When I reached the Metropolitan area I crossed the Brooklyn Bridge on the footwalk. At the Brooklyn end I ran into an ex-patient, an alcoholic who could hardly stand up. He flipped when he saw me. Anyway I moved through the streets in Manhattan into the East Village area where I got some temporary help from a hip couple and then proceeded toward the west Village where I ran into Boy Holst the Hobohemian, as he then called himself. Boy was always a very kind person and he took me to the Living Theater on Fourteenth Street. We met Julian Beck and Judith Malina and I poured out my pleasure at meeting them. They immediately involved me in some stagehand work for their current production and gave me a bit of bread for some food.

Unfortunately, or fortunately, depending on your social philosophy, I wound up back in the Long Island place shortly thereafter.

There was a footnote to the escapade, however. I received in the hospital mail call a copy of the current Living Theater playbill, listing my name as a stagehand.

A GENERATION AGO

It was as normal and American a development as the seventh-inning stretch that there should have been a Beat Generation after World War II. There was a Lost Generation after World War I, so why not? The great battles over, Verdun in the first war and Stalingrad in the second, one peered with interest at the slackness, the looseness, the coolness, the mutedness of a strangerdom á la Meursault. Lucien Carr killed Kammerer in a murder involving homosexuality. Crimes depending on minute individual quirks rather than great abstract issues. Relatively insignificant issues captured the imagination, insignificant people, ambiguous people of uncertain motives replaced great heroic monoliths of declared noble purpose. "I don't care." "I'm beat." Instead of important words that one hung upon, instead of this, came a playing with words.

So I met Allen and, as a further gratuitous occurrence, Allen, it turned out, knew Lucien. Not only Allen, who is perhaps a bit more well-known than he deserves to be—but, for example, Gerd Jack Stern, who, in our great postwar get-together, turned out to be the nephew of Abraham Stern, leader of the Stern Gang of Jewish terrorists. Gerd had a poet-friend named John Hoffman from Menlo Park, California, and the two of them shipped out on a Scandinavian ship around 1950. John was a spaced-out type who called everybody "Man" as did Gerd. He was not very interested in hard work and this attitude was very common in those days. When the Captain of the ship asked John to bring him soup, John misunderstood and brought the Captain a bar of soap. John had a girlfriend named Karen and went down to Mexico shortly after the soap incident. He caught mononucleosis down there and died in his early twenties.

To me, this whole old story of postwar beatnikry is very old hat. It occurred, it had to occur, was natural and normal as apple pie (including the "madness" bits which certainly should have been expected from a generation steeped in Kafka exegesis) and it is a mystery to me why there should be, at this time, a whole literary sub-industry devoted to research on the Beat era, or "movement" as it has been called by some. Granted that this whole phenomenon took up most of my time. What else was there to do?

(As a footnote to this chunk of writing on the postwar generation of mid-century, I am at this time wondering what happened finally to Jean Genet. I have seen no mention of his life and work since he last turned up at the 1968 Democratic convention. I see his name used frequently in crossword puzzles as "French playwright," but that is all. Where, oh where, is the fabulous "Voleur," the marvelous sorcerer of prose-poetry, who was the subject of so much hagiolatry in the time of our youth?)

There is a wholly different cast of characters on the world stage at the present time and I feverishly work my brain trying to keep up with exploits of characters as diverse as Bjorn Borg, John Irving, and Bobby Halpern—as well as trying to acquaint myself with whatever remaining classical writers I may have missed out on in the past (like Rabelais, or reading more about Baron Charlus).

Nevertheless, the industry of beat research and Kerouac biography continues to chug along.

As I write about the romantic aspects of the beat era, I suddenly recall the less romantic aspect of "madness," seldom if ever referred to in the recondite avant-garde magazines who create rapscallion heroes and legends by the dozen—that is, very specifically, the high cost of the various therapies which our intellectual needs and flamboyancies led us into. For the very rich, therapy is a matter of minor expense, but for others, of middle- and low-income groups, having disciplinary problems in a college and winding up in a long siege of psychotherapy (lasting years) can be financially disastrous. It's expensive to be crazy, so please be considerate and think twice before you hang a "crazy label" on someone not in the best circumstances money-wise.

The money matter has dogged me all along and still does. Although intellectual styles may change from generation to generation, remember that there is no psychological or metaphysical malaise that cannot be instantly cured by the gift of one million dollars in cold cash. Would Jean Genet have been Jean Genet, with his "twisted" and "degenerate" mind, if he had been brought up in the Rockefeller household, say, and would he not have had the normal mind of the late Governor? And might not the reverse have been true if . . . ? So before you stand up with judgmental condemnations of beats (many of whom worked hard and paid taxes for much of their occasionally marred lives) might it not be wise to make allowance for certain social evils (there are victims of circumstance, William Buckley or Marie Antoinette) before you impute a supernatural demonism or disease to our minds? And further, in appraising certain of the companions of my younger days one should know that most, including myself, have learned with age to proceed with some caution and have engaged in multitudinous shifts of habits, attitude, and ideology in the years that have ensued.

Take even the apparent nihilism of Camus' choice of subject in Meursault. It was not endorsement of Meursault's act. It was more a visualizing of the subject ("if there were such a man or such a crime") accompanied by a sharp implicit criticism of the stranger's failure to embrace the Sisyphus-like morality of Dr. Rieux in *La Peste*. The "notorious" label of existentialists, beats, hippies, and perhaps punks on into the present, stems more from the flirting with such thoughts rather than actual performance. Is it condemnable to think dangerous thoughts? Remember Philip Nolan in *The Man Without A Country*, who for a momentary verbal lapse suffered a lifetime exile. Allen is always, still, flirting with dangerous thoughts. He would think it intellectually "chicken" not to. Should I have jumped ship in France in the forties? Having learned from my mistakes, presumably, now I would say I should not have jumped ship in the forties. But then I would have learned nothing of Artaud and the body of avant-garde literature that I did learn about as a result of that ill-famed adventure. I would have been like other college English majors, pure in my following of a college curriculum and might now be teaching snugly in some college. Maybe a little of both caution and rashness is good. I don't need to jump ship again. Now I can read all the required books at home in my leisure hours. Perhaps the ultimate result may be a better alloy.

While it is true that the greater part of the intellectual ferment we experienced as a group began shortly after the war, the older members of my original generation have been living out their lives with better or worse results, through the later years. Max Dumbrow, a Trotskyist or socialist leader on the Brooklyn College campus in the late forties, known affectionately as "Mad Max," died last summer on Fire Island of a heart attack. Certainly unknown to all of us personally, but an ominous, intellectually forbidding Pope of the New Criticism whom some of us read, Allen Tate, died last year. Beauford Delany, black painter friend of Henry Miller, familiar to readers of Miller's earlier work, died in a French mental hospital also last year. Neal Cassady lived out his life and died in '68, but only last year I stood in a Manhattan subway station and there confronting me on one of the metal poles was the graffiti, "Neal Cassady lives." Of the super-intellectual ferment of 1950, when being very highbrow and supererudite was in high fashion, little remains but what seems to me the cropping up of epigone movements like structuralism and whatever new mental health fad each new season brings. A thoroughgoing dwindling, though not an utter dying-out, of the original naive enthusiasm, madness, and involvement. What later work by Michaux, for example, can compare for sheer novelty and genius with the early postwar *Un Barbare En Asie*? What Yippie gyration in anarchism can compare with the sheer drama of Artaud's outcries in his last days? Not that there is not much of intellectual sustenance in the present turmoil. Our current intellectual figures are well-schooled and magnificent reasoners; controversy about Eurocommunism, the great amount of thought being devoted to the enigma of homosexuality, all make interesting reading. But, for me at least, it is all somewhat subdued and no great discovery or turn-on like my postwar encounter with surrealism and the rest of it.

Comparing the deaths of two Presidents while still in office, I remember being moved by great sadness at the death of Franklin Roosevelt and more by shock and surprise at the death of John Kennedy. These deaths occurred 18 years apart—about one generation—and in the difference between the two reactions one can spy the difference in intellectual and emotional texture between the two eras.

Where to begin in this chronicle? Better just to write without regard to organization of the data and impressions. Elise's suicide: This Jewish girl from Columbia was around the Yorkshire Residence Club on Morningside Heights where I lived after my divorce from Olive. She was seriously concerned about helping me toward mental health, since my somewhat eccentric lonerness (stemming I think from being an only child) always seems to worry groupies whom I befriend. Anyhow, from the Yorkshire to the State Hospital was a short jump and while I bided my time in the hospital, Elise came with Allen and Peter to see me. Her kindness and human warmth were hard to reconcile with the later news: that she had done herself in as a result of later developments in her life and psyche. Joyce Johnson, who was also around the Yorkshire scene at the time I was, later wrote about Elise and her suicide in a novel called *Come Join The Dance*. Sixties, yes sixties.

Suicide and homosexuality became two obsessive post-World War II themes. Weldon Kees, avant-garde poet, parked his car, in about 1948, on the Golden Gate Bridge and apparently took the Big Leap. Gore Vidal rose to prominence with *The City and the Pillar*. Apocalypse, corruption, disease became obsessive themes and continue epigone-fashion as generation follows generation and overlaps upon the one that preceded it.

Madness in high places began with Forrestal and his Big Leap and continues with doubts of Nixon's and/or Carter's sanity (the *Caine Mutiny* theme worked and reworked and each time apparently successful in eliciting a shocked response). Madness in low places á la Artaud and your neighbor's granddaughter.

Shall I tell what I know of the story of Bill Heinie

(walk around town in any decade and you'll pick up reams of such data)? Bill Heinie was hanging around with Huncke and the two names sounded like a very funny comedy team when mentioned together: "Huncke and Heinie." Heinie, around 1967, had a reputation as a black magician. Whether he actually practiced voodoo or something similar I do not know, but I was continually being told around then to stay away from Heinie, who to me seemed a benevolent enough hippie type. The result here, and the last mention I ever heard of Heinie was that he had been declared insane and was being sent to Matteawan —Matteawan no less! He had somehow contacted Allen and angrily demanded the services of a lawyer.

The old school crowd. Talk of my generation. A generation, one should realize, does not merely include its most colorful, notorious or illustrious members. It also includes the non-flamboyant ones who have lived their lives in relative obscurity. I have been running into some of these since my return to the city in 1964. They take pride mostly in their parenthood or even grandparenthood and dote on the accomplishments of their children or grandchildren. They know me again for my slightly eccentric (aw, call it original) poems and essays of high school days.

DEDANS L'ASILE PARMI DES FOUS

Voids, misery, beatniks, exiles, I have become so redundant since my first little experiment in Dada. The audience demanded a repeat performance so enthralled were all the little termites with my first romantic gesture. Kirilov in the form of Carl Solomon continues to thrill you with his death-defying antics. Rigaut said "Suicide is a vocation." When I was a little boy I never knew what I should become. Every profession or real role seemed a tomb. Trotsky, Tshombe, Lumumba, Job. Gratuitous acts, Zen and Vitalism. Hipsters, Jesuits and Abbott and Costello. Look, I will explain the whole thing to you. The paramount fact is that I am bored with the colorlessness of everything. So we made a hero of Willie Sutton during the fifties. Heh, heh. Remember the Mad Bomber. The basketball scandal. Christine Jorgenson. We have to find something somewhere. The whole world is closing in, nothing new in anything. We are being bored out of existence. Point two. Ginsberg is nuts and everybody is secretly nuts. Not one damned thing since I was born apparently has had any significance. Wasn't World War II a bore. Why do you want to read this? So I'm some type of schizophrenic who lies on the floor of a ward and smokes cigarettes made of newspapers and Cayuga State Tobacco. I laid off sex for six years and while I was doing so the San Remo vanished as a point of reference. Now I'm thirty-three and exactly the same. The same detached appearance.

AGE: 36

Even as I said I had belief nobody would believe me and I would still have no belief.

Nobody knows what anybody else is talking about and all conversation, even war, is conducted merely for the sake of argument. Arguing at least lets us feel that truth, the slippery eel of an object, is open to contention and will be the reward of the stronger arguer. "I think," "You think" . . . As if there were anything to think. I have never seen a thought, either a free or a censored thought and doubt whether any such things exist. But I have seen bodies, of all shapes and sizes in all sorts of positions and predicaments and would now define free thought as a body sitting on a park bench. While censored thought I would conceive of being a body in a straitjacket.

What I'm trying to do now . . . see, I'm letting you in on my latest con . . . is just to sit around the house and grow flabby around the waist, watch the news programs and take walks. I don't know why you should call it a con but it probably is.

The dadaists thought they had something with suicide. I have something much greater with non-suicide. Try non-suicide. The big kick here is when somebody else commits suicide and you don't. I have a number of these little gimmicks lying around the house. Like non-maladjustment, non-defeat, non-rebellion, non-beatness, and non-hipness.

I read the newspaper items on various types of non-conformists having legal difficulties with great relish as I have no legal difficulties. The world came to an end for me a long time ago. I bequeath to posterity my discarded comas and hallucinations. And thank God (?) nobody will ever again (forever) scream the screams I have screamed or weep the tears already wept. Hold on, there will soon be new tears to weep and new screams to scream. There will be screamers as long as the world goes on and there must always have been screamers in the past.

Hey, literary public, how many one-eyed whores do you want me to screw in the eye? I was Lautréamont a long time ago and now am only a psychiatrically disabled ex-ice-cream salesman whose life history can be figured out by nobody. I get tired thinking of all the bums I have transcended, of all the cretins I have out-punned, of all the pénetrating exegeses I have spun out to deaf mutes. Have a heart, even if they're gonna put a stake through it some day (see Guy Wernham trans.).

Didn't Ginsberg and I go through all that nonsense about Dostoyevski some 15 years ago and then it was about 300 years old. What do you want me to say? Moo? Goo? Or moo goo gui pan?

A DIABOLIST

Perversity in all forms appeals to those who desire a new reality. The quintessence of evil suddenly seems desirable because you are bored with "What's new?" and "How do you do?" Of all poets, the perverts seem most interesting.

Turn off the ball game. Do something odd. Run a bath and stay in for three hours, or talk to an odd-looking man you meet on the street. Then you are on the path of what certain writers call the marvelous. The end is dementia praecox. What you have been seeking is absolutely dementia, a seclusion room by yourself or a straitjacket all your own. This because you desired to turn things around to make the ugly beautiful. Such alchemy is not a pretense and is not limited to one writer. It is domain on which any daring individual may trespass. It has existed for many centuries. And the unusual says Lautréamont is to be found in the banal. The extraordinary is to be found where you sit. I cannot break the fascination with this view of life, call it the bright orange view as opposed to the grey view.

This is better than a hobby; it is almost the equivalent of a religion.

I shall make up a dream I never dreamed and you may explore it for significance. I was sitting on a beach; a dog came up to me and licked my leg; a fat boy came by; he wanted to play ball. It seems that we played ball for years. Then the dream ended. What a silly dream!

Sometimes the diabolist regrets his sins against nature and dreams of gods or reality. But reality persists in being boring.

Who can understand my odd nature. My passion for the absurd or the prank. I live for these things. I have traveled and travel is a flop so far as I am concerned. Wherever you go you are a tourist, that is to say some sucker to the odd denizens of the place. Give me my home, my imagination and my dreams.

It is almost as though the "real" world were an asylum and the unreal world is a super-asylum . . . for those who have gone insane in the outer madhouse and been placed in this outer void. It is a place where those who don't know they are insane are placed. Those who know they are ill are outside consulting psychiatrists. Pilgrim is the sort of place you leave by asserting that the correct date is actually the date and the correct man is actually the president. There is a definite letdown in being released . . . you feel upon leaving the Insane Asylum as though you are entering the Sane Asylum.

This all is a task too difficult to describe once you have attained this dimension. It is like hearing the inaudible . . . seeing the invisible.

LOLLIPOPS

Young girls swept like a whirlwind into the store, devouring giant lollipops. They had bought them somewhere in the neighborhood. When they left, they said, "Goodbye, darling." Things can't be all that bad if little girls devour giant lollipops and say, "Goodbye, darling."

RECOLLECTION OF AN INTERESTING INTERLUDE

Before? After? Who knows? Here's a fraction of time, and that's my strength, I'm going to draw its outline, and capture its intonations, and recreate its scent a little. The nation mourns the death of Martin Luther King, headline the dailies. The local atmosphere, the global atmosphere, et cetera, et cetera, they all blend together, and from all these "atmospheres" is born the vigilant wait. I am waiting, amongst other things, for a telephone call about a job. My health is good. I still have some food left, and a roof. I'm not growing. I'm not trying very hard, but the moment could come. . . . The flounder are in. That I know. I was on the pier a few days ago, and I caught five of them. Two big ones and three little ones. I gave them to a colored lady who hadn't caught anything. How grateful she was! It was the very day after King's death. A certain miasma surrounds that whole story. We had known that for a long time but, like you, I don't want to go into details. It's a miasma that I vaguely noticed a few years ago in reading Camus' *The Fall*. That was probably the most depressing of all his books. The story takes place in an Amsterdam dive, and the general tone implies that it is already too late, for a lot of things, but that at least we can conceal our desperate state of mind beneath a verbose mask of charm. Listen, I'm bringing our day to light. Watch out for verbiage and charm. They conceal a pretty desperate state of mind. So what? At least, with a little luck, I can recreate the whole situation, with a few spicy details, and *that's* art.

A MOMENT IN FRONT OF THE LIBRARY

The willingness to stop. So stop. The crowd gathers. The Marxist seems to be benevolent, he sometimes draws crowds in this neighborhood, involved yet again in debate with a patriotic black. Subject: the situation in general.

He's got enemies and a few sympathizers. Suddenly, a thought comes to me. Why haven't I seen any deaf and dumb people in these parts for so long? A few years ago, downtown was packed with them, scurrying around here and there, happily, in little groups. Have all the deaf and dumb people disappeared by now? In any case, the Marxist wants to set up a government in exile. What? Right in the middle of the street? Yes. That's what he wants. I am not eating sweets any more. Too much trouble with my teeth these last years. The time has come to be forceful. Make a resolution and stick to it. Ignore the government in exile. Could it improve the state of my mouth? Both sides seem to have good arguments. I look at the two speakers, smile vaguely when everyone starts laughing. I don't know what to think. I don't want to get involved. After a period of respectful attention, I move on. Yes, it could be that there's something wrong with the Ukrainian nationalists. But the same goes for the Marxists. A good speaker can make a bad impression on anybody, if his arguments are disorganized. The tide rises and recedes. I remain skeptical about everything. Nothing decisive can come out of this confusion. Even so, it did me good to listen. The Marxist really did avoid that question about Stalin's daughter, and skillfully. I miss the deaf and dumb people.

WHERE I'M AT AND LOOKING BACK

Well, the Mets have made it and that's, sure as anything, the end of the sixties. I was lugging laundry bags with E.K. near the beginning of this decade. We were discussing Ed Kranepool, the James Monroe graduate. The Kennedys were much in the spotlight. Somewhere on the periphery of our consciousness were Tshombe, Mobutu, Kasavubu, and Lumumba. It was apocalyptic as usual. As apocalyptic as it always seems to seem, you generally improvise, rationalize and stumble through. Not everything that could be desired, but you make it. Not Kerouac. Answer? Simple. He drank too much. If you feel, or let other people make you feel that it's not worth watching anymore, the big amorphous, protean scene, there are ways out. As for me, the encouraging thing is the noise the crickets make in the lot near my house in the springtime. They chirp away and I feel renewed, thrown back to Nature Study classes in public school and class picnics amid the wooden benches of Pelham Bay Park, still standing and just across the street.

Yes, George Montgomery, I ran around with you to Yankee Stadium and to Barnegat Bay and I was a famous Sick Man and everybody was trying to cheer me up and we had all the mimeographed magazines and there were Le Roi Jones and Hubert Selby and literature assumed to me a strange form. Well, this is where we're at and everybody is being mentioned in everybody else's autobiography and Jack and Neal are no longer with us and Ginsberg is still an excellent and searching conversationalist. Whoooo!!!

November 1969

POETRY IN THE SEVENTIES

Somehow gone as magically as they came are the days when, with enormous interest and excitement, I consulted those obscure French *revues* in the 42nd Street Library, reading critics like Max-Pol Fouchet on "young men of twenty" and George Bataille "on laughter" and Henri

Pichette's tributes to Artaud. And the image of Artaud himself, turning words into volcanoes or something or other (to believe the tributes). And those shocking pictures of Artaud (no end of them) looking like a man who had been rolled by the universe while drunk. Gone as magically as they came. Now talking about inflation and recession and lifestyle and worried about layoffs. Yes, on a Wednesday evening I can, if I feel energetic enough, go down to St. Mark's on the Bowery for the latest get-together of the Poetry Project. Nothing cataclysmic: nothing to shake one up. Sometime normal-looking poets and sometimes someone like Gregory who simply strikes me as funny-looking. Then, on the job, in my book department of the department store—where we sell lots of Kahlil Gibran's wisdom and enjoy sudden runs on the poetry of any poet or poetess (preferably poetesses) whose suicide has recently been reported in the paper or on TV (like Ann Sexton). My feeling is that poetry isn't where it's happening just at present.

February 12, 1975

ASSOCIATING WITH CLASSY PEOPLE

Reacting sharply to one of my remarks, my old Marxist buddy says to me, "You always were basically middle class." I feel desperately hurt. I argue in the bar, "If you did the work I do, all the heavy lifting, instead of just sitting behind a desk and spouting theories, you wouldn't call me middle class." He says, Marxist academician to me, semi-shipping clerk, "I'm not condemning the American workers, I am merely condemning certain of their attitudes." This conversation stemmed from the difference between our attitudes during the Vietnam War. I've been, for a number of years, half-swallowing the populist rhetoric of the American right, finding it comfortable and salubrious. It gives me a slightly uneasy sense of well-being. So I shut up. We finish the evening together without any more serious feeling or conversation. I go home.

Arriving at my home in the Bronx, I say to my mother angrily, "He condemned me as being middle class." "Middle class," says my mother. She's hurt too, but for a different reason. "What does he mean—middle class? You have *more* money than he does. *He's* middle class and you're upper class."

Suddenly, I dig the humor, seeing the semantic difference in the use of the word *class* by left-wing intellectuals and the common run of Americans. The one refers to ideology and the other to the amount of money you have in the bank.

February 16, 1975

WORK DAY ENDED—1976

Far from the world of Petronius Arbiter and its Manhattan replicas, far from the world of bizarrie and gaga literary glamour. Far from all that, at least in the fact that my mind did not focus on it in the work day just concluded; far from all that, I have just expended some effort of limb and of concentration to gain for myself 32 dollars. Writing this little attempt at prose creation makes me a somewhat more fortunate individual I think than Artaud who, at a similar age was very likely writing his letters from Rodez, where he would die at 51 or 52, I am not sure which. My work lacks Artaud's tragic grandeur (which I hope will never be mine) but it does attempt a description of a fairly interesting experience. In the morning, I set out in an express bus (air-conditioned) from my rather quiet middle-class (lower ?) neighborhood and enjoy a pleasant ride through the Bronx, across the Harlem River into Harlem, through Harlem, and along Fifth Avenue beside Central Park. We pass the Metropolitan Museum of Art, many monuments, a lake, a zoo, and a baseball field before we reach the Manhattan shopping area where I work in a large department store.

The work day begins with punching the clock. It comprises a period operating a computerized cash register, waiting on customers, unpacking books, and rendering some assistance to the housewares department in placing on its sales wall all manner of items imported from Taiwan: egg-poachers, melon-ball cutters, meat-tenderizers, etc., and not quite ad infinitum.

The day ends with punching the clock once more and taking the subway home from 42nd Street. I generally read the *Post* on the train and think considerably about the columns of Max Lerner, James Wechsler, and similar adepts in the field of socio-political commentary. By eleven o'clock, if I have had a tranquil day, I am generally asleep. I thank you.

SITTING AROUND TALKING ABOUT THE GOOD OLD DAYS

Go, my life! The memories flow in crowds. There are so many of them that, often, if you simply stop talking, you cackle like an old man. Names like that of Harry Gumbert, relief pitcher for the old Giants, come out of nowhere to fill up my head. And Cliff Big Ears Melton. And Monte Pearson. For this you need some old buddies who can also remember these things. Of course, I don't live completely in the past. I take an interest in the exploits of Willie Mays and Yaz and of players of today. I don't know why, but I was hurt when Ruth's home run record was broken. My mind has started to look like one of those "time capsules" that they're selling at the libraries these days.

MANY PORGIES, MANY FLOUNDERS, A FLUKE, A BLACK, A SNAPPER, AND AN EEL

Fishing around City Island has picked up. The Lebanon War has been forgotten and some readers have switched to the supermarket newspaper *The Star*, where they read stories about babies covered by warts and Siamese twins with maple syrup in their veins. My fishing friend, Jack, contenting himself with domestic pursuits this year, talks yearningly of a trip to Atlantic City. We have been fishing with Lucien Carr and we have been a very effective piscatorial trio—not to mention Lucien's friend, Clifton, who has also fished with me. We have really been knocking the flounders dead this year and, Sunday, I amazed even myself by catching a 16- or 17-inch fluke. Fishing and doing the crossword puzzle and jumble are my big ego-boosters in the psychologically debilitating Armageddon-conscious atmosphere. Read one masterfully written commercial-type novel by Moravia, *1934*, which corresponds, strangely enough, with some of my recent reading and thinking. He deals with both Kleist and Seneca-type stoicism and damned if both Kleist

and Seneca haven't been among my more recent acqui-
sitions. To ask about the state of affairs in NYC you have
to be joking unless you have a much stronger stomach
than me. It would be nice if the White Sox won in the
American League West this year because they haven't in
such a very long time (1960?). I see Mayor Koch occasionally standing on the steps of City Hall, presiding over
some festivities or other and he is taller than I thought.
As a messenger (present gig) I run all over town and my
favorite places are the air-conditioned high-rise construc-
tions and the chirping, cheerful people in them. What
else is worth communicating to you? Saw some funny
Japanese in a rowboat Sunday, laughing and talking about
eating fish raw if they caught any. I identify with the *Jaws*
Captain Quint. Six and a half years to Senior Citizenship.
Is that interesting? A young audience would go bananas
if they had to depend on reading me, because my greatest
pleasure in life just now is eating green pea soup. When
you've reached the outer reaches of longevity the air indeed becomes pretty rarified. Inanity in yourself is harder
to recognize and isolate. Sometimes you are and you don't
even know it. I am still young enough to say it's a very
funny feeling. But there's no other direction to go in than
becoming older each year. I can't become younger each
year, now, can I?

SOLOMON TAKES A BATH

What a relief, muses Solomon, as the lukewarm water
washes off the sweat of the day's honest toil.
"I am Sweeney, Sweeney taking a bath," he imagines.
His career in ruins—his ruins beginning a new career

(he had visited the Acropolis in 1947 and is sure some interesting use will be made of the Acropolis in this the Computer Age).

Solomon-Oblomov lies down on his bed and shouts out, "Zakhar, more *KVASS*!"

Solomon-Charlus smacks his lips as he reads this week's *Village Voice*.

Solomon-Pierre muses again over what he heard Sunday night in a lecture at Theosophy Hall.

All this time, Solomon, C. Wolfe Solomon, or Sea Wolf Solomon, has been wondering how such a huge complex marvel as this day has come about.

May 24, 1983

HOBO JOE DIDN'T SURVIVE AND WHY

Some people augured the early eighties as the new dark age. Others said it was the computer age. Or the age of high-tech; or the age of Reagan. Anyway it was to be a tough period. According to all the pundits. In my part of the Bronx, we argued much, among ourselves, over whom was to be the most likely to survive the forbidding age to come. Such arguments were very heated and became a rather painful but a favorite indoor sport.

Hobo Joe had been in the printing line but hadn't held a job in years. He was a veteran of Guadalcanal, according to himself, and vaunted his own toughness continually—toughness at survival in the cold, master of tricks and gimmicks, ladies' man, killer of at least one Jap on Guadalcanal. Schweinhund (I won't use his real name —he survived—) was a young kid, a sensitive neo-Nazi, subjective and given to moodiness. Hobo Joe victimized Schweinhund to a certain extent, borrowing sizeable sums of money from him and not repaying. In the bargain, Hobo Joe ridiculed Schweinhund's efforts to survive. "Not tough enough," proclaimed Hobo Joe. "I'm still a young man," pleaded Schweinhund. "I'm too young to die." "You'll never last on the street," insisted Hobo Joe. What he said to me at the time carried a similar message. I was coughing my lungs out then, with a thirty-year-old smoking habit. I sadly agreed Hobo Joe might be right.

As it turned out, now that we are entering, according to the current issue of *Time* magazine, a new age of compassion in these the late eighties, Schweinhund and I survived and sit sometimes reminiscing about the defunct Hobo Joe. He'd been tough all right, but he hadn't checked out his cholesterol and had died of a heart attack several years ago. I've given up smoking and my lungs are clear. Schweinhund is still a neo-Nazi, but somewhat mellower and keeps a tighter hold on his purse strings.

March 28, 1987

IV
SANITY AND THE SANITORIUM

LETTER TO GOVERNOR ROCKEFELLER

My dear Governor Rockefeller,

I am a patient who is awaiting official release from Pilgrim State Hospital. I am now on convalescent care.

I want to register a complaint against the totalitarian know-nothings prevailing in this State among the general population.

I returned to this benighted country from France in 1948 and was promptly attacked as crazy in immediate milieu for reading Baudelaire, wearing sandals and talking French. I have been given insulin shock treatment and electric shock treatment for no reason that is apparent to me except that I do a little translation and reading. I was deprived of my union book by the National Maritime Union for having been a member of the Communist Party in the early forties when I was 15 years old.

This and countless other abuses in the interests of illitjeracy and I am sure, indirectly, in the interest of Stalinist antimodernism have been perpetrated on me by the boring squares who seem to be the same in all countries whether Russia, Yugoslavia, or the United States. I plan to leave for the Carpathian Alps when I am given my official release, that is to say permission to re-enter this degenerate community. In the Carpathian Alps I will settle down with a few other initiates and read Kropotkin while evading the cold gaze of Ana Pauker. I am content that I am the American Mayakovsky and have been all but suicided by the society (read *Van Gogh, The Man Suicided By Society* by Antonin Artaud).

As a lover of the arts as myself, what do you suggest in the way of rehabilitation, re-orientation, etc.? I believe I have a great deal to contribute to society. In what way can my great talents be utilized? I am wasting away in an uncreative milieu, a quasi-criminal milieu and being treated like a parasite by my conformist but bountiful family which also *madly* still regards me as a communist because I left home at seventeen when I was still that. I have no personal resources. And I have no interest in any commercial outlets. The poem "Howl" was written in my honor by my friend and fellow patient at the New York Psychiatric Institute, Allen Ginsberg. As far as my own writing is concerned, read "Afterthoughts of a Shock Patient" in the anthology *The Beat Generation and the Angry Young Men*. I need little magazine attention or attention of some kind. Do you have any magazine connections that could use a dark horse contributor?

Your friend,
Carl W. Solomon
Sunday, February 25, 1962

PILGRIM STATE HOSPITAL

One enters Pilgrim as though it is the deathhouse. One sits down in the ward and waits. Five doctors approach, the patient weeps.

Shock treatment is prepared. One wakes dazed.

Allen comes, he says, "Don't argue with them, do as they say."

Time asserts itself again. You go home. You tire yourself out sleeping with women. Then you pause. You think, "You are a writer, you should do something again."

It is tiring to understand what they are saying to you, you talk about Nerval and you talk about Proust.

A young man comes up to you. He is of Arabian descent. He mentions Nasser and begins an anti-Semitic diatribe.

Dr. Rath is a young man. Of Romanian-Jewish descent. A background more brilliant than any doctor in the institution so far as I am concerned.

You mention Tristan Tzara to him and he understands what you mean. He works through group therapy. Patients come together and remorselessly cut each other to pieces. Fights break out during the course of the group therapy session.

"Solomon, you don't want to get well. You're just looking for a big dick." I fight back, I knock the boy down. He screams, "I'll kill him even if they send me to Matteawan."

He had disclosed to me in an earlier conversation that he knew Weinberg, slayer of Bodenheim. "Bodenheim was gay," asserts Davis.

I disagree, not being quite sure of my facts.

Come back to Village years later and find Bodenheim's reputation as a man was quite good. Davis escaped from Pilgrim. I don't know what happened to him, hard-bitten and bitter, I have never forgotten that face. Dehumanized.

Confused him in my mind with Corso since both had reformatory qualities. Met Corso again—changed my mind. Corso is a littérateur and a Catholic with a strong religious sense of right and wrong.

The tendency toward crime among the young men of my generation is impossible to surmount. We are all guttersnipes. Gratuitousness is the spirit of the age. Gide and Cocteau have made us what we are. The big dick or *bite* if you prefer me to use Genet's French, this is all that matters. Make another man submit to you and you are God.

Ah! Ludicrous ribaldry. (Hemingway) blowing his beautiful understanding face to ruins with a bullet. Camus dead in an auto accident.

Of all things, Artaud becomes vogue ten years after his death as a ridiculous nut.

Berchtesgaden. The Fuehrer and his blond boys, who is this man Castro? Very late on the scene. New young communist intellectuals in the Village, a new group, a new element very much involved in politics.

Why, I don't understand them. They are good men.

Kennedy seems quite human after all that has occurred. Maybe he will restore some kind of dignity to my life. He has begun already. He appointed a Jew to the Cabinet.

He himself is a Catholic, an enormous advance in democratic thinking on the part of the American public. Democracy versus nihilism in daily life. Motivation or despair.

THE ABYSS

(A story of philosophy and mental illness)

I wasn't sure which it was this reality or the other one. And then there were so many realities, the reality of Frank in the clothes-room and the reality of the dandies in Paris. Each one riding his own drunken boat. And I am buffeted between these separate worlds and cannot explain the relationship between them except through a wild stare. There is Sam's reality, Sam whom I met in another madhouse, Sam and his marijuana, and the supermarket shopping reality of my mother who rescued me from this madhouse. Nothing seems to add up and still I have gone on all these years, laughing and happy despite each wacky impasse or change. I suppose I am lost though temporarily at least found, and talking to you. And it is not so terrible to be lost, let me assure you, escaping from nuthouses, sleeping in cemeteries, selling ice-cream, being alternately a good guy and a bad guy. The only trouble is that it all happened in a vacuum and nobody knows where I was or why it all happened.

Thank God at least (you do call on somebody) that the violence of my emotions has been tempered by either time or the tranquilizing pills they gave me. There are no more hallucinations, no more voices, no more pressure on top of the head and behind the ears, no more shouting on my part.

TORTURES OF THE DAMNED

Preamble

This is not a last word. Nor is it a first word. It is not even a cough. It is not even a murmur. But let us be straight with each other, you are afraid of me and I am afraid of you, all coughs, yawns, and polite smiles to the contrary. You are afraid of me because you know that if you are smaller, less athletic, less apt than I am I may attack you and you will have no recourse but to let out a weak cry: "Help!" I know that if you are bolder, bigger, or uglier than I am, the slightest dissenting remark about politics, sex, religion, or art will put your hand around my throat or your toe to my groin.

THE SULLIVANIANS AND OTHERS

Once I sought help from this brand of psychiatry. As I remember, the doctor was vague and sympathetic. While seeing him, I read Riesman and thought much about status problems. He had me turned on for a while. Under his gentle hand, I turned from a *bete noire* to a fashion plate. However, he ultimately betrayed me. He wondered why I was taking him quite so seriously. Therapy ended with a violent dispute about irrationality. Under his guidance, I was one week a Zen Buddhist, the next week a Socialist. Perhaps he loves me still, I do not know as I no longer see him. Unprecedented success with women seemed the main end-product of this form of therapy. Since I stopped seeing him I have been somewhat unsuccessful. I don't know what it was. Perhaps he cast an aura about me that fell off when I stopped paying him. Then came the hospital doctors, in great variety. These were for the most part pill-pushers. I remember one who called me "Charles" which is not my name. However, they were kind enough not to detain me for the rest of my life. Hypnotists, spiritualists, and tarot fortune-tellers, also literary critics and poets have been my advisers concerning the most intimate matters. I feel that I am doing well when the Black Muslim standing on 42nd Street smiles at me for buying a copy of *Elijah Speaks*.

WALTZ YOUR WAY TO FREEDOM

(Memoir of mental illness)

I am free again . . . that means well again. Against a background of newspaper *coups d'etat*, pop art, and unreadable poetry one makes one's way into the Real realm where one may comfortably park under a tree reading a copy of *Mad* magazine in comparative safety. Now that I am on the outside I wonder about the sick ones I knew and where they are and what individual manifestos they are writing. At the hospital dance, miscegenation danced side by side with bad grammar.

There is no issue in this business of madness and sanity, so there is nothing to fight about. Only individuals with a thousand separate answers. Dropped here and there on a Douanier Rousseau vista of open country.

The century of fantastic art must produce a fantastic audience and fantastic sensibilities.

I am now fairly up to date again, and I can recall the hospital staff with some familiarity and affection. Yes, affection. There are some fighters and the fight goes on in these places continually. I imagine it depends on the stage of rehabilitation that you are in to determine whether you are a fighter or cooperative.

The culture tells one to fight, fight, fight. Yet, in the hospital you are better off if you walk away from a fight. There it is that you learn not to fight, to learn the lesson of understanding rather than the lesson of fighting.

From the land of the Hivinizikis back to America.

I stood on the ward and pointed at the moon and told one of my simpleminded cronies that there was a man on the moon.

ARTAUD

I witnessed an Artaud reading in 1947, the year before Artaud's death in Rodez ["*Je suis mort à Rodez sous l'électrochoc*"]. in 1948. Artaud was being described by a small circle of Paris admirers, some in very high places in the arts, as being a genius who had extended Rimbaud's vision of the poet-seer. His name was even described by one admirer, known as "the Alchemist," as Arthur Rimbaud without the HUR in Arthur and without the RIMB in Rimbaud. And this man later made a case for Artaud as being, literally, the reincarnation of Rimbaud and spiritually his descendant. Other admirers were André Gide and Jean Louis Barrault. Gide made a case for Artaud as an existentialist man of despair, and Barrault had been influenced by Artaud on the theater. Artaud's is a tenuous case, an ambiguous one in that he has been highly esteemed by almost everyone of note in the arts and yet widely banned and condemned by legal authorities.

To me his case, his destiny has been the cause of considerable confusion since one knows that by accepting his theories one puts one's body in the social frying pan and by rejecting him you are going through life with blinders on. He is certainly the leading critic I have ever read of social hypocrisy and for this became known as a "damned" poet. He was a junkie, a lunatic and had pursued his peculiar turn of thought so far that he had even rebelled against surrealism which itself is supposed to be rebellion against society deriving from a rebellion against the "rebel," Anatole France, who had been considered too lucid, too rational, by the early Dadaists. And where does all this rebellion against rebellion lead but surely into one of many large nuthouses which are continually being constructed all over this country and others in the name of that mystical cause "Mental Health."

The book by Artaud which impressed me most was his *Van Gogh* written in 1948 in which he condemns all forms of psychiatry, and thereby all organized authority, since all countries practice psychiatry including the socialist wonderland. In it, he claims that every lunatic, everyone marked and branded, and believe me all lunatics are really marked and branded, is a person of superior lucidity whose insights society thinks disturbing to it. This book impressed me when I read it in 1948, the year of Truman's upset victory over Dewey. I was still in the school system at that time and the intellectual students, by these I mean the ones who weren't in favor of basketball and who read a book now and then which wasn't on the compulsory reading list, were mostly interested in either Marxism and folk songs or, in the advanced echelons, in Freud or Wilhelm Reich. Now I was interested in Artaud, who to me was a symbol of real rebellion truly inheriting the name.

To illustrate the mood of the student body in college at that time, I should state that I walked into a classroom carrying a copy of Baudelaire and was immediately latched upon by a girl English major who seemed to think I was actually Baudelaire in person. Shortly after this I was deposited in a nut factory where I was shocked into a renunciation of all my reading, etc., etc. What books remained to me after I had been shocked there, were later stolen from me by various local hoodlums and I was soon thrown into another more savage nuthouse.

The case of the so-called lunatic opened up by Artaud and no other writer is really the case of Socrates, who was condemned to death for being what, in his day was considered "bright," that is to say not stupid. I say that we live in a generation of charlatanry, propaganda and corruption, and that there is no room for an honest man on either side of the Iron Curtain.

RAMBLINGS

I first came upon the concept of the void in Artaud and also in the book by Husser, *Phenomenology*. However, it is not a word which occurs in everyday speech, so I dropped it subsequently for the purpose of communication. As you may recall from reading Artaud, he built a hard shell of nonsense et cetera around him to avoid rational discourse. This is an attempt to shelter oneself from unpleasant contact. It really embraces the various methods of being "*uncooperative.*" Any type of deep retreat into the self or into the realm of the absurd fits into this category. It is renunciation of social obligations and duties.

A PLEA FOR ZERO

"Honesty is the best fallacy"

I believe in the zero of zero of zero
Because I want to be without ideology.
I am only a man among messiahs
And have been deceived by Stalin, by Isou, by
    Reich.
Only by Artaud are we not deceived,
By the idea that language is merely gabble,
That one would do better to chew gum perpetually
    than to talk.

A FEW NOTES ON WHAT HAS BEEN HAPPENING TO MY SOUL

God, the Devil, and at least half a dozen angels figure strongly in what has been occurring over the last several years. Against a background of rising Castroism, several battles between heavenly angels and horny devils have

been fought and won, of course, by the legions of para-
dise. A lot of booze has been drunk, a lot of Salvation
Army hymns have been sung, several acts of sodomy have
been committed and a number of floozies have been in
and out of love with me, as their hungry stomachs dic-
tated. We cannot do without this earthly parody of heavenly infernal combat, so let us at least eat our blintzes in
silence.

THE LUNATIC AND MODERN ART

"Le Seul Vrai Langage Est Incompréhensible"

... Artaud, "Ci-Git"

With the theories of Antonin Artaud, not his earlier
works like *The Theater and its Double*, but with his later
postpsychotic works like *Van Gogh, The Man Suicided By
Society*, the artist as a productive member of society is
thrown overboard and Artaud-le-momo (or Artaud the
Nut) emerges as hero of art and letters. Sub-normality
and sub-reality are the theme and tone of the late Artaud
and his followers. For Artaud and for Genet and even,
to an extent, for Michaux, and for the Lettrists, neolog-
isms, screams, belches, and the passing of wind are sub-
stituted for the written word.

Ridiculous as all this sounds, it has actually existed
as a post-war trend in painting as well as in literature (in
the *art brut* of Dubuffet and others.) Call it latter-day Dada
and you are well.

There is actually a literary tradition to back up this
sort of thing. If you are a poet who had read late Artaud
and wishes playfully to experiment, you are apt to be
bound up in a straitjacket by the nearest psychiatrist and

given no credit for your research until you get a scholarly article on the subject published in the *Partisan Review*.

Dada is dangerous today because the police, among others, don't understand what it's all about (being readers of the *News* and not of the *Partisan*, let alone of *The Evergreen Review*, or even of *Poetry* or even of *Time*) and probably mistake you for the dumbell you are attempting satirically to mimic.

To avant-garde poets, nay, extremely avant-garde poets, let me state that the *flics* of 1964 shoot first and do exegesis later.

For all of Ginsberg's fun-loving tone in "Howl" (which was written for the author of this article) and for all of Kerouac's and Lamantia's and Corso's funlovingness, let me state that I am not serious and have never been serious about anti-literature.

I was first of all a student of English at Brooklyn College when a mild "Ping-Pong of the Abyss" episode occurred at the NY Psychiatric Institute in 1949, and renounced all that to make good grades and to start over. But so intrigued were my local fans with the fun of going into a hospital and asking for a lobotomy that they forced me into the absurd role of lunatic-saint again and I could never get my much yearned for degree. Now I am released from a much more terrifying hospital and can't get a job or a degree (so much time has been lost, I am now 35 and hardly an enfant terrible).

The upsetting fact is that I am a writer and not a paranoiac and go by Mann, Proust, and Eliot more than I do Artaud.

Somehow the legend of my "*infirmity*" built up, is still building up, it is by this time documented by Department of Mental Hygiene records, fingerprints and photographs.

I am quite willing to renounce Dada, sub-normality, etc. but the ridiculous Art vs. Society war still rages in the pages of the *Evergreen Review* and elsewhere and I can't seem to get a hearing.

This is a situation that Kafka would have handled well.

Am I to renounce literature and hope for a job as a messenger boy with weak nerves?

I would love to. But I can't get it. I am still rejected at this time by job placement personnel who regard me as too intellectual.

The bureaucracy, here, in Russia, and in the neutralist countries, demands identification. Who are you? Where were you on such and such a date? Do you love your mother? Your fingernails show dirt. Your breath is bad. Do you like girls?

And I have lost my credentials. I liked a girl but she left me for another man. Was she of good character? I thought so in the beginning.

REPORT FROM THE ASYLUM

Afterthoughts of a Shock Patient

A book that is accepted, at the moment, as the definitive work on shock therapy concludes with the astonishing admission that the curative agent in shock treatment *"remains a mystery shrouded within a mystery."* [Hoch & Kalinowski, *Shock Therapy*] This confession of ignorance (and it is extended to both insulin and electric shock therapies), by two of the men who actually place the electrodes on the heads of mental patients at one of our psychiatric hospitals, certainly opens this field of inquiry to the sensitive layman as well as to the technician. The testimony that follows is that of an eyewitness, one who has undergone insulin shock treatment and has slept through fifty comas.

One may begin with amusement at the hashish-smokers and their conception of the sublime. They, who at the very most, have been *high* consider themselves (quite properly) to be persons of *eminence* and archimandrites of a *High* Church. A patient emerging from an insulin coma, however, cannot help being a confirmed democrat. There can be no hierarchization of different levels of transcendency when they are induced by an intravenously injected animal secretion, the very purpose of which is to bombard insulin-space with neutrons of glucose-time until space vanishes like a frightened child and one awakens terrified to find oneself bound fast by a restraining sheet (wholly supererogatory to the patient, since, in the waking state, spaceless, mobility seems inconceivable). The ingenuousness of the hashishins is stupendous.

It is as though the Insulin Man were to call his drug by a pet name and spend days thrashing out the differences between *gone pot* and *nowhere pot*.

The difference between hashish and insulin is in many ways similar to a difference between surrealism and magic. The one is affective and is administered by the subject himself; the other is violently resisted by the subject (since this substance offers not even the most perverse form of satisfactions); it is forcibly administered in the dead of night by white-clad, impersonal creatures who tear the subject from his bed, carry him screaming into an elevator, strap him to another bed on another floor, and who recall him from his *reverie* (a purely polemic term employed in writing *down* the hashishin). Thus, insulin comes as a succubus, is effective, suggests grace.

In this respect, the paranoid fantasies released by hashish lack substantiality and are of the nature of automatic writing or gratuitous acts. In the case of insulin shock therapy, one finds oneself presented with a complete symbolism of paranoia, beginning with the rude awakening and the enormous hypodermic needle, continuing through the dietary restrictions imposed upon patients receiving shock, and ending with the lapses of memory and the temporary physical disfigurement.

Early in the treatment, which consists of fifty hypoglycemic comas, I reacted in a highly paranoid manner and mocked the doctors by accusing them of *amputating* my brain. Of course, my illness was such that I was perpetually joking (having presented myself to the hospital upon reaching my majority, I had requested immediate electrocution since I was now of age—how serious was this request, I have no way of knowing—and was discharged as cured exactly nine months later, the day before Christmas).

Nevertheless, I noted similar paranoid responses on the part of other patients in shock.

For those of us acquainted with Kafka, an identification with K. became inevitable. Slowly, however, the identification with K. and with similar characters came to imply far more than we Kafkians had ever dreamed. We knew it to be true that we had been abducted for the most absurd of reasons: for spending hours at a time in the family shower, for plotting to kill a soldier, for hurling refuse at a lecturer. And, in this particular, the text had been followed quite literally. The need for a revision of the Kafkian perspective arose, however, when the bureaucracy suddenly revealed itself as benevolent. We had not been dragged to a vacant lot and murdered, but had been dragged to a Garden of Earthly Delights and had there been fed (there were exceptions and there is a certain small percentage of fatalities resulting from shock, making the parallel to grace even more obvious). This impression arose, somehow, from the very nature of the subjective coma.

Upon being strapped into my insulin bed, I would at once break off my usual stream of puns and hysterical chatter. I would stare at the bulge I made beneath the canvas restraining sheet, and my body, insulin-packed, would become to me an enormous concrete pun with

infinite levels of association, and thereby, a means of sur-
mounting association with things, much as the verbal puns
had surmounted the meaning of words. And beneath this
wrathful anticipation of world-destruction lay a vague
fear of the consequences.

The coma soon confirms all of the patient's fears.
What began as a drugged sleep soon changes organically
and becomes one of the millions of psychophysical universes through which he must pass, before being awakened by his dose of glucose. And he cannot become
accustomed to these things. Each coma is utterly incom-
parable to that of the previous day. Lacking a time sense
and inhabiting all of these universes at one and the same
time, my condition was one of omnipresence, of being
everywhere at no time. Hence, of being nowhere. Hence,
of inhabiting that Void of which Antonin Artaud had
screamed (I had been conditioned in illness by classical
surrealism).

Invariably, I emerged from the comas bawling like
an infant and flapping my arms crazily (after they had
been unfastened), screaming, "*Eat!*" or, "Help!"

The nurses and doctors would ignore me, letting me
flap about until my whole aching body and my aching
mind (which felt as if it had been sprained) pulled themselves by their bootstraps out of the void of terror and,
suddenly, attained a perfectly disciplined silence. This,
of course, won the admiration of the dispensers of grace,
who then decided that I was eminently worth saving and
promptly brought me my breakfast tray and a glucose
apéritif. And in this manner, item by item, the bureaucracy of the hospital presents the insulin *maudit* with a
world of delightful objects all made of sugar—and gradually wins his undying allegiance. If we are not deceived
by appearances we will see clearly that it is the entire world
of things which imposes itself upon the would-be *maudit*
and eventually becomes the object of his idolatry.

All told, the atmosphere of the insulin ward was one
in which, to the sick, miracles appeared to be occurring

constantly. And, most traumatic of all, they were concrete miracles. For example, I am reminded of the day I went into a coma free of crab lice and emerged thoroughly infested (the sheets are sterilized daily). I had caught the lice in somebody else's coma, since these states of unconsciousness are concrete and are left lying about the universe even after they have been vacated by the original occupant. And this was so credited by one of my fellow patients that he refused to submit to the needle the next day out of fear of venturing into one of my old comas and infesting himself. He believed that I had lied and that I had crabs for some time, having caught them in some previous coma.

Meanwhile, on that following day, I was revived from my coma intravenously by an Egyptian resident psychiatrist, who then, very brusquely, ordered the nurses to wrap the sheets around me a bit tighter lest I should free myself prematurely; I shrieked, "*Amenhotep!*"

And there was the day a young patient who had given the impression of being virtually illiterate, receiving his intravenous glucose (one is revived from a deep coma in this manner), and then gave ample evidence that he had become thoroughly acquainted with the works of Jakob Böhme in the course of his coma. Simone de Beauvoir, in her book on her travels in America, expresses her consternation upon finding that a member of the editorial board of *Partisan Review* once openly admitted to being ignorant of the writings of Böhme.

Shortly after my mummification and defiance of Amenhotep, I encountered what appeared to be a new patient, to whom I mumbled amiably, "I'm Kirilov." He mumbled in reply "I'm Myshkin." The cadence of the superreal was never challenged; not one of us would dare assume responsibility for a breach of the unity which each hallucination required.

These collective fantasies in which we dreamed each others' dreams contributed to the terror created by contact with the flat, unpredictable insulin void, which had not yet been rendered entirely felicitous (as it was to be later) by the persistent benevolence of man and glucose, and from which all sorts of incredible horrors might yet spring.

The concomitants of therapeutic purgation were, for me, a rather thoroughly atomized amnesia (produced by an insulin convulsion of a rare type and occurring in not more than 2 percent of cases) and a burgeoning obesity caused by the heavy consumption of glucose. Much later in my treatment, when intensive psychotherapy had replaced insulin, both of these phenomena came to assume places of great importance in the pattern of my reorientation. As my illness had often been verbalized, the first effect of the amnesia was to create a verbal and ideational aphasia, from which resulted an unspoken panic. I had quite simply forgotten the name of my universe, though it was also true that this name rested on the tip of my tongue throughout the amnesiac period. All ideas and all sense of the object had been lost temporarily, and what remained was a state of conscious ideational absence which can only be defined in clinical terms as amnesia. [So great was the sense of tangible loss that I later insisted upon an electroencephalographic examination, to reassure myself that no organic damage had resulted from the convulsion.] I had been handed, by skilled and provident men, the very concrete void I'd sought. During this period, I had gained sixty pounds, and upon consulting a mirror, I was confronted with the dual inability to recognize myself or to remember what I had looked like prior to treatment, prior to reaching my majority.

When I had recovered from my amnesia sufficiently to find my way about, I was permitted to leave the hospital on Sundays, in the company of a relative of whom I would take immediate leave. My relatives on these occasions seemed entirely oblivious to any change in my behavior or physique. Generally, still rather hazy, I would be escorted by an old neurotic friend to a homosexual bar where, I would be informed, I had formerly passed much time. However, the most appalling situations would arise at this point, since, in my corpulent forgetfulness, I no longer remotely resembled a butch fairy or rough trade. I had lost all facility with gay argot and was incapable of producing any erotic response to the objects proffered me.

Almost imperceptibly, however, the process of object-selection began once more in all realms of activity, and gained momentum.

I amazed my friends in a restaurant one Sunday afternoon by insisting that the waiter remove an entrée with which I had been dissatisfied and that he replace it with another. And even greater was their incredulity when they witnessed my abrupt handling of a beggar, this having been the first time that I had ever rejected a request for alms.

> "The yearning infinite recoils
>   For terrible is earth"
>
> —Melville, "L'Envoi"

At about this time, I wrote a sort of manifesto, called *Manifest*, which is a most pertinent artifact:

Corsica is an island situated off the coast of Sardinia. Its capital is Ajaccio and it is here that Napoleon Bonaparte was born. Though it is a part of the French Empire, Corsica is not part of the mainland. It is an island. As Capri is an island, and Malta. It is not attached to the European mainland. I am in a position to insist upon this point. There is a body of water separating the two, and it is known as the Mediterranean Sea. This is borne out by the maps now in use. I brook no contradiction. If I am challenged on this point, the world will rush to my assistance in one way or another. What I have just written is a standing challenge to all the forces of evil, of idiocy, of irrelevance, of death, of silence, of vacancy, of transcendency, etc. And I rest secure in the knowledge that my challenge will never be accepted by that *Scum* to whom I've addressed it. I've spent considerable time in the clutches of the *Loon* and I've waited for this opportunity to avenge myself by humiliating the void. Thank you for your kind attention.

—A Vehement Adult

As the business of selection became increasingly complex, I appeared to develop an unprecendented (for me) suavity in operating within clearly defined limits. Madness had presented itself as an irrelevancy, and I was now busily engaged in assigning values of comparative relevance to all objects within my reach.

My total rejection of psychiatry, which had, after coma, become a final adulation, now passed into a third phase —one of constructive criticism. I became aware of the peripheral obtuseness and the administrative dogmatism of the hospital bureaucracy. My first impulse was to condemn; later, I perfected means of maneuvering freely within the clumsy structure of ward politics. To illustrate, my reading matter had been kept under surveillance for quite some time, and I had at last perfected a means of keeping *au courant* without unnecessarily alarming the nurses and attendants. I had smuggled several issues of *Hound And Horn* into my ward on the pretext that it was a field and stream magazine. I had read Hoch and Kalinowski's *Shock Therapy* (a top secret manual of arms at the hospital) quite openly, after I had put it in the dust jacket of Anna Balakian's *Literary Origins of Surrealism*. Oddly enough, I hadn't thought it necessary to take such pains with Trotsky's *Permanent Revolution* and had become rudely aware of the entire body politic I had so long neglected when, one evening, I was sharply attacked by the head nurse of the ward for "communism." He had slipped behind me on little cat feet and had been reading the book over my shoulder.

The psychiatric ineptitude of the official lower echelons became incredible when, one week before Halloween, it was announced to the patients that a masquerade ball would be held on the appropriate date, that attendance was to be mandatory, and that a prize would be given to the patient wearing the "best" costume. Whereupon, the patients, among whom there was a high spirit of competition, threw themselves precipitously into the work of creating what, for each, promised to be the most striking disguise. The work of sewing, tearing, dyeing, etc., was done in Occupational Therapy, where, at the disposal of all, were an infinite variety of paints, gadgets and fabrics. Supervising all this furious activity was a pedagogic harpy, who had been assigned as Occupational Therapist to see that we didn't destroy any of the implements in the shop (she tried to persuade me to attend the masquerade made up as a dog). Furiously we labored, competing with one another even in regard to speed of accomplishment, fashioning disguised phalluses, swords, spears, scars for our faces, enormous cysts for our heads. When Hallowe'en Night arrived we were led, dazed and semi-amnesiac, into the small gymnasium that served as a dance floor. Insidious tensions intruded themselves as the time for the awarding of the prize approached. Finally, the social therapists seated themselves in the center of the polished floor and ordered us to parade past them in a great circle; one of the nurses sat at a piano and played a march; to the strains of the music, we stepped forward to present our respective embodied idealizations to the judges. There were several Hamlets, a Lear, a grotesque Mr. Hyde, a doctor; there were many cases of transvestism; a young man obsessed with the idea that he was an inanimate object had come as an electric lamp, brightly lit, complete with shade; a boy who had filled his head to the point of bursting with baseball lore had come as a "Brooklyn Bum," in derby and tatters. Suddenly the music stopped; the judges had chosen a winner, rejecting the others: we never learned who the winner had been, so chaotic was the scene that followed. There was a groan of deep torment from the entire group (each feeling that his dream had been condemned). Phantasmal shapes flung themselves about in despair. The nurses and Social Therapists spent the next hour in consoling the losers.

Thus I progressed, after my series of fifty comas had ended, and finally reached my normal weight of 180 lbs. and my true sexual orientation: adult heterosexuality (which became my true sexual orientation only after the basic androgynous death wish had been redirected). It is probably true, however, that my case is atypical and that the great majority of such transformations are not quite as thoroughgoing, and in some cases, fail to materialize at all. There were those patients who were completely unmoved by the experience of the coma, and who found that it did nothing more than to stimulate their appetites. And there were those Kafkians who remained confirmed paranoiacs to the bitter end.

I should like to quote a passage from an article by the French poet, Antonin Artaud, published posthumously in the February, 1949, issue of *Les TempsModernes*. Artaud had undergone both electric and insulin shock therapies during his period of confinement which lasted nine years and terminated with his death in March 1948.

> I died at Rodez under electroshock. I say died. Legally and medically died. Electroshock coma lasts fifteen minutes. A half an hour or more and then the patient breathes. But one hour after the shock I still had not awakened and had stopped breathing. Surprised at my abnormal rigidity, an attendant had gone to get the physician in charge, who after auscultation found no more signs of life in me.

I have my personal memories of my death at that moment, but it is not upon them that I base my accusation.

I limit myself to the details furnished me by Dr. Jean Dequeker, a young intern at the Rodez asylum, who had them from the lips of Dr. Ferdière himself.

And the latter asserts that he believed me dead that day, and that he had already summoned two asylum guards to instruct them on the removal of my corpse to the morgue, since an hour and a half after shock I still had not come to.

And it seems that at the very moment the attendants appeared to remove my body, it quivered slightly, after which I was suddenly wide awake.

Personally I have a different recollection of the affair.

But I kept this recollection to myself, and secret, until the day Dr. Jean Dequeker confirmed it to me on the outside.

And this recollection is that everything Dr. Jean Dequeker told me, I had seen, not this side of the world, but the other . . .

What he describes above was the experience of us all, but with Artaud and so many others, it stopped short and became the permanent level of existence: the absence of myth represented by the brief "death" was accepted as the culminating, all-embracing myth. Artaud went on to write, in his essay on Van Gogh, that a lunatic

is a man who has preferred to become what is socially understood as mad rather than forfeit a certain superior idea of human honor

and to write further that

a vicious society has invented psychiatry to defend itself-
from the investigations of certain superior lucid minds
whose intuitive powers were disturbing to it

and that

every psychiatrist is a low-down son-of-a-bitch.

In Paris, quite outrageously, this heart-rendingly skewed
essay written by a grieviously ill man was honored with a
Prix Sainte-Beuve and was underwritten by several of the
most distinguished French critics.

I have a small mind and I mean to use it.

The sentence above epitomizes the real lesson of insulin, that of tragedy, and it was neither written nor would
it have been understood by Artaud, who remains (he
wrote that *"The dead continue to revolve around their corpses"*)
a sublime comic figure, one who averted his eyes from
the specter of reality, one who never admitted to having
dimensions or sex, and who was incapable of recognizing
his own mortality. (In the list of comic figures of our time
we can include the homosexual.)

My release from the hospital was followed by a period
of headlong and vindictive commitment to substance, a
period which continues, which is full of tactical and syn-
tactical retreats and rapid reversals of opinion. It is obvious by this time, though, that the changes of opinion
are becoming less frequent, that the truculent drive toward compulsive readjustment, toward the "acting out"
of one's adjustment, has been dissipated. My attitude toward the magic I've witnessed is similar to that of the
African student I met a month ago, who told me that his
uncle had been a witch doctor. He had seen his uncle
turn into a cat before his eyes. He had simply thrown the
uncle-cat a scrap of meat, hadn't been particularly impressed by the magic (though conceding its validity), and
had come to America to acquire the political and tech-

nological skills with which to modernize his country upon his return.

For the ailing intellect, there can be great danger in the poetizing of the coma-void. Only when it is hopelessly distorted and its concrete nature disguised can it serve as material for mythmaking. To confront the coma full-face, one must adhere to factual detail and this procedure need not prove deadening. On the contrary, the real coma administers a fillip to one's debilitated thinking processes. Jarry's debraining machine was not the surgeon's scalpel but was contained within his own cranium. It was to place the coma thus in context that I undertook this examination of its architectonics.

FURTHER AFTERTHOUGHTS OF A SHOCK PATIENT

At our house, we have frankfurters pederaste.

Frankfurters pederaste consist of corn niblets, pimentos, and frankfurters sliced fine and fried.

Of course, we brook no contradictions.

We eat quietly, discussing the war when we feel impelled to do so. "I think they'll win," says she.

I ignore her remark and go on eating, knowing that if I dispute this point the world will rush to her assistance.

We've accepted the tragic.

Meanwhile, at an Automat table on 42nd Street, a hashishin finishes his coffee and stretches wearily, sighing, "Life's a drag."

The gang of deaf-mutes at the adjacent table, having

read his lips and misinterpreted *comme toujours,* elects a delegate to reprimand the boor.

The delegate accosts the hashishin. He is the most articulate of the mutes and speaks, at best, in a spastic manner.

"They—aaaa want you—aaaa to apologize—aaaa!"

His chest swells. He's proud of his little speech.

The hashishin opens an eye and grimaces, "Too much!"

A skeptical instant and the delegate conveys the hashishin's *apologia pro vita sua* to his comrades, each deafer than the other. Stealthily, three of them rise and slip out of the cafeteria. They've already conferred. No gestures, but a glance. With dispatch, the delegate strides back to the hashishin's table.

"They—aaaa aren't satisfied—aaaa! Go outside—aaaa and face—aaaa them like a man—aaaa!"

In a subway car, three hashishins sit eating tarts.

All at once, the door between the car and its neighbor bursts open, spewing forth forty deaf-mutes, all jubilant. They converge on the hashishins. The hashishins cast about, frantically seeking succor. The legitimate passengers in the car ignore them, staring stolidly at the advertisements. A station! Like a herd of bison, the mutes snatch the tarts from the hands of the hashishins and rush through the opening door out onto the platform, laughing silently.

Later in the day, the depredations of the mutes, who desire a senseless society, increase.

Dinner gone, I busy myself with my translations, while she tosses in bed violently, waiting for me to retire. Generally, we're both asleep by eight o'clock.

I am translating Rimbaud. After hissing, "*Je suis un Negre,*" he rants on the screech, "*Jesuis un autre.*" Refusing to be taken in by an infant of nineteen, I translate. "You're another." She tosses.

* * *

No such thing as prophetic humor.

A young hashishin visits the leader of the hashishins at his apartment, seeking more hashish.

The leader of the hashishins tells him, "I don't push no hash no more. I push blossoms now."

The Italian war-cripples riot in Rome, trampling bipeds, plutocrats in space, beneath their crutches, parallelling, in a special way, the riots in England following the adoption of the Gregorian calendar, when the citizenry burned the Pope, plutocrat in time, in effigy, over their eight purloined days. The dogs insist upon having their days and a world in which to roam, to boot.

The dugs of the heroes of Bataan grow longer, requiring bigger and bigger brassières to contain them.

I pause in my translation of Rimbaud to think of my wife, whom I hear tossing in the bed behind me.

With her in mind, I re-peruse a news dispatch which intimates that the heroes of Bataan have, as a result of nutritional disorders suffered at the time, sprouted breasts within the year, breasts which secrete.

I think of Napoleon Bonaparte, who had left Ajaccio a slim and virile youth only to acquire feminine characteristics upon attaining the heights at Austerlitz.

I had rejected heroism the year before; I breathe deeply, eternally grateful.

The mammaries of the heroes of Bataan grow longer and longer.

"*Dereglements des sexes*," my text seems to read. I find it exceedingly difficult to get on with the translation.

I'm thinking of her as she continues to rustle in the sheets behind me, trying to lure me into bed.

* * *

What can be clearer? Eliot, snickering over his foot-bath at the dugs of the sissy seer, Tiresias.

I attempt to return to my Rimbaud, both hero and seer, ever overweening—did *he* wear a brassière?

I snicker at the tits of the heroes of Bataan, and get on, at last, with the translation, thankful that I am a man and not a woman.

Meanwhile, the breasts of the heroes of Bataan grow longer and longer, but the nipples remain the same, secreting no more, no less, than ever.

Who wants to be weaned by a hero of Bataan?

Outside in the falling dusk, a falling "transient" wraps his body in an evening newspaper's front page, which is entirely black, but for a tiny headline sacrosanct in white, "YANKS WIN! 7–1." He throws himself to the ground, behind the park benches. He falls asleep easily. Passersby avert their gaze, suspecting or hoping that he is dead.

Time to retire. I put the translation aside, undress and walk to the bed on tiptoe. She awaits me with open arms.

"Has baby finished with his nasty writing?"

I pause on the verge of dream, hesitant.

My dream, too, will be functional, eminently livable. I continue.

LETTER TO DR. RATH

My Dear Dr. Rath,

It goes without saying that madmen are really mad. As you may or may not know, when I first entered Pilgrim, it was through the back door of the psyche more or less. The domination that I felt was not that of the hospital, society or authority, but that of the gonest patients. Psychologically, spiritually, even physically, the hierarchy seemed reversed. I broke with the guidance of my friends, the doctor, the writers, because psychologically I became aware that night was real and not day (see this as clarity or obscurity.) I did this because more and more I had noticed the tendency on the part of the professionals (we shall call my friends in whose rational vision I had lost faith *The Professionals*) to confess sham in their social world, to say, "All right Flaubert, but those boys, even though they're mad, they really have powers—the elemental powers." Their tendency to apotheosize the primitive. The contemporary writer or painter feels secure in so far as he basks in the approval of the Bantus. How could I respect them—well, I say now that I was mistaken. It was a nauseating vision and a completely homosexual one. And it is wrong to disapprove of homosexual vision. Yet in modern times, homosexual writing, in all countries reaches the bestial level (Genet, Williams, Bowles, Burroughs) and preoccupies itself more with the carnal aspect of what had always been conceived of as a philosophic attitude. Instead of yearning for immortality as Plato did, the modern homosexual philosophers yearned for death, violent if possible. Carnality obscured clarity and the contemporary bourgeois classes lack self-esteem. They become stilted and create a fantastically stratified society to substitute for the existence of a real power or authority. They can't curb delinquents, they can't curb the Mafia, the French can't crush the Arabs, their children don't respect them anymore, they are obliged to make pacts with the Communists in wartime—so they create the illusion of other-directed conformity to substitute for the old individualist ideal in bourgeois thinking. Since our society doesn't exist anymore, we had better make out like it does by all imitating one another. He who does not imitate is lost, he who is lost does not exist, because we are creating the illusion that we all exist in a kind of mirror reflecting mirror-togetherness. Naturally it is rather difficult to respect a society which pretends it exists or to respect yourself if you are a member or a symbol of it. The stilted imitativeness of the other-directed archtypes, the men in the grey flannel suits, the population of *White Collar* or *The Lonely Crowd*—the lonely ones are really looking around for someone to imitate (consider—the man in the grey flannel suit—he is in advertising where the hero used to be an inventive or eccentric impressario bursting with ideas), this stiltedness is obviously less of a force capable of winning and holding respect than any old Bantu or madman, free-swinging, etc. When you exist in the eyes of the other-directed, your existence is a precarious one, particularly when in the streets or in a madhouse—because these professionals, in their other-directedness, with their grey flannel suits, try to look only at one another, pretending that the delinquent toying with his zip gun or the Arab fondling his knife (I could name others, but I shan't because you've already heard of some such types from—enough said) don't exist, and are certainly not a substitute for the old-fashioned executive type who could promise you law and order. So you have the picture, a society which can't defend itself from its internal or external enemies finding a temporary solution only in conformity—not in religiousness but in conformity. The reason why I surrendered other-directed status was that I felt its weaknesses. These people (the professionals) can't defend themselves from the forces destroying their own society—what a weak faith my faith was. Ortega's *Revolt of the Masses* is about it. The social structure is weak. My working with interpersonal relations was no defense against The Street, where interpersonal relations are not recognized, where people exist in namelessness and facelessness, presenting only primitive masks—some people. The situation has nothing to do with politics.

I like things here at home because it provides me with a certain measure of safety. Can you find time to reply?

V

EMERGENCY MESSAGES

WHY NOT BAN MODERN ART?

Since 1870, with the beginning of the symbolist
and the impressionist movement, humanity has been
tortured by these crazy poets and meaningless painters.
Today they cram the asylums of the world flinging in-
sults at doctors and potato salad at lechers. These gyp-
sies roam over the world like lice threatening suicide
and doling out ambiguities. The city, nay, the world now
reeks of marijuana and hashish. Political degeneracy and
paranoia are everywhere. They wear masks, these flip-
pant nobodies, speak to Irishmen with a brogue, Jews
with an intonation, and social workers in the words of
Lombroso, they often work as policemen so that one
can no longer tell if the policeman is a criminal or the
criminal is a policeman. The last will of Dr. Mabuse
has been carried out. Order has been completely sub-
verted. A mockingbird hangs over us from an hallu-
cinated limb chirping atonally. Beria has been shot as
a spy and well whadda you want me to say. This is the
day of the monkey.

We, poor simpletons have been gulled. I think it's
time we took the so-called law into our own hands and
blasted these pettifogging sophists into the infernos they
have imagined. Why not proscribe prose altogether and
insist, nay, scream, that they talk like corny people, like
us. Jean-Paul Sartre, for one, ought to be burned at the
stake right in Paris, France, for talking like an idiot.
Whadda they want us to do, hold up stores, commit bank
robberies, and give up our fun, which constitutes playing with box tops. Well, I, Mr. C. Solomon, editor, lecher,
pervert, fink, dadaist, and lunatic declaim, nay, assert,
in the face of this tribe of "sports," as they fancy them-

selves, that I prefer playing with box tops to holding up banks.

Perhaps you ordinary folks will join me in this protest against current reign of abstract destructiveness.

Joe Doakes

DISASTER LOOMING

Just left an important package in a taxicab. There must be no slip-ups. Am I cracking-up again? Is my pleasant, soothing grip on reality slipping again? No. There are definite steps I can take. Notify the police. All lost items must be reported. There shall be no crack-ups, no slip-ups. The police will help me. The package will be found. Or replaced. Regardless of the general malaise, the package will be found or replaced. I must have been thinking of something else when I should have been thinking of the care of the package. Never do that, in spite of the multiplicity of distractions in the city. Always keep your mind on the task at hand no matter how menial. These trifles cost heavily when they are used against you. I must have been thinking of writing a poem about Big Ears and Dickey Bird. Why go so far afield in the search for material anyway, with ordinary middle class living exciting, yes breathtaking enough these days? I will rest one day, two days until the harrowing matter of the package is resolved one way or the other.

EMERGENCY OVER

Ah! What a relief! The emergency is over. The package, I have just learned, can be and, in fact, is going to be replaced. There was no emergency at all. I was worked up over nothing. These days that happens. People get worked up over nothing at all, some trifle, and begin trembling and looking agitated. There was nothing at all to be agitated about. What a relief! Ah! What a relief. Nothing at all to be agitated about. Quite simply a tempest in a teapot. Ha! ha! ha! I shall now lean back, light myself a firm new cigarette and laugh at the world. Yes, learn to learn to laugh again. To laugh at the world, as I should. Ha ha! Ha ha! Ha ha ha!

TRAFFIC ROARING BY

But I like to write about knights on chessboards and stirring deeds of madness and magic. Have I learned something about reality? "Yes, I see dux." "No, Carl, those are not dux, they are trux." I lie on my bed and listen to the traffic roaring by. I know it will never stop. Is this what I have to write about, the dull sameness of experience? Yes, Mary, I would like some mint jelly with my roast leg of lamb. Americans who are really waitresses and truck drivers and carpet cleaners? Yes, this reality. And the reality of sex which all the good writers of my generation write about. The normal truthful, humdrum thing in which the great writers have always found poignancy, a poignancy which lies beneath the surface and is hardly obvious. I finish my leg of lamb and I go upstairs. My uncle has gone out. The bell rings. A woman seeking a tenant I do not know. I can't take it for long, not this overpowering normalcy. Before a week is out I will be searching for the surreal again. Just something a little unusual. Maybe a new East Village antic or publication to ridicule, not to devour but to ridicule. I noticed the same stirring with the brief Arab-Israeli War as with the Kennedy assassination. A sudden stirring. Makes the heavy monotony seem like a game. Like play in which there are winners and losers or a puzzle in which a hidden object may be found. Well, somehow, we jazz it up. Like looking at a cop and wondering which branch of the John Birch Society he belongs to. Like the girl I know who says "grass" instead of "pot" though she doesn't use it. Just to jazz it up. Like Kerouac's rhapsodies over the banal. Really the banal. Ball games and jazz musicians and soupy love affairs. Like strange hairstyling for men and kooky costumes and perversions. Just to jazz it up. My girlfriend complains that I'm not romantic enough. I remind her of Stanley Kowalski. I wonder if I should wear a cocked hat and get a mandolin. Call it the Great Society and have happenings. But it's the same old thing a bit jazzed up. Uptown, downtown, trying to add some differentiation to the dull appallingly monotonous terrain, to the buildings and the traffic. Yeah, yeah, yeah. The same old drag. It takes both stick-to-itiveness and imagination on this terrain. The first to last through the lags in interesting events, the second to be able to respond when they occur. Until the next time. Yeah, yeah, yeah.

CONFUSED, GUTTERAL MUMBLING OF
A MAN WHO HAS READ TOO MUCH

Kafka,
Strindberg,
Jack London,
Gogol,
Mike Gold,
Edward Everett Hale,
Heywood Broun,
Westbrook Pegler,
Jacques Vaché,
Henry Miller,
Stalin,
Mao Tse-tung,
Hitler,
Mussolini,
William Buckley,
Lawrence Ferlinghetti,
These and many, many more,

And what have I gained in the way of everlasting wisdom?

Nothing.

Literature has nothing more to offer one than the many blank faces one meets on the subway ... it is of course only a way of killing time or a subject for conversation. Is this giving away the game?

But cannot this be said about anything ... baseball just so many batted balls? Where is what I am looking for? And is there anything I am looking for?

Let us say: I read to keep my hands occupied ... to keep from masturbating.

I am possessed of language and have nothing to say.

Why not collect postage stamps, dirty jokes, or puns?

Drinking endless cups of coffee or entering a pie-eating contest makes about as much sense.

I am somewhat disappointed in Ferlinghetti. The true Dada would have been to have gone across Russia on horseback.

A NOTE ON TRANSMIGRATION OF MY SOUL

Enough said for this brief lifespan. However, I now take this opportunity to serve notice upon Allen Ginsberg. [Since his abandonment of the true Dada, I have christened him "Vasco Fiasco."] Claude Pelieu and any other friends I may miraculously have made in this life (the one beginning in 1928—not the one in which I was Richard the Lionhearted) that in my next life I am going to come back as a very high official in the 21st-century American State Department and that it will take enormous sing-outs, sit-ins, etc. to quell my unconquerable spirit.

REACTION TO READING THE FALL BY CAMUS

Very good. The beautiful, calming, sensuous prose. The world takes on the hue of the Amsterdam barroom where the action is set. The narrator's tone becomes my tone. Sometime in the late fifties, in the hospital of course.

That's where I was when I read *The Fall*. In the world of raging action, this prose seems to transcend the action, to stop it for a moment. Later, we discuss. During the weeks which follow the reading, discussion of it intermittently occurs. Years later, somebody with whom I had discussed it when I appeared, a young painter (a knowledgeable young painter) says to me, "Carl, you know now it appears to me that the existentialists are crooks or seedy bums." True. One would get that impression from gazing upon the characters whom their philosophy seems to extoll—the Irrational Men—the nuts. There are so many interpretations of this philosophy that I can't settle on an answer; nor can I settle on an answer to the existentialists' continual debate with both the Marxists and the Catholics and perhaps the Freudians as well. Maybe they are all right and Ginsberg as well. I pause and think, "After some few years it will all be over for me. All I have to do is plod along for a little while longer and then it will all be over. The goddamned disputations will end. They'll all be dead and silent—great philosophers in their time. Didn't Carl Sandburg write, 'I am the grass. I cover all.' "

LETTRISM

Lettrism was and is a Paris-based poetry movement which appeared on the French literary scene during the years immediately following World War II. Its founder was a Romanian-born Jew named Isidore Isou. His real name had been Goldstein, but he had changed it to Isou, which is a term of endearment. In an endeavor to assimilate to French culture, somewhat mockingly perhaps, he occasionally used the name Jean Isidore Isou. Among his principal disciples was a young poet named Gabriel Pomerand. The major magazine conveying this movement's poetry and body of theory was called *La Dictature Lettriste*. The movement is little known in America and was mentioned mostly in Joseph Barry's Paris letters during the various periods following World War II. Isou's obvious similarities to Tzara (Romanian birth, etc.), the timing of the movement's inception, its poets' use of nonsense words and similar pyrotechnics, and the similarity of their poems to the utterances of people suffering from the psychiatric illness known as echolalia—all caused the Lettrist movement to be characterized as neo-Dada and to be laughed off as such, almost disregarded when compared with movements of richer and more involved content like Surrealism, post-Surrealism, Existentialism, etc. Isou himself, in his writings, seems a complete egomaniac claiming to be (himself) the direct descendant of a line beginning with Mallarmé and Rimbaud. His principal work, *Une Nouvelle Poesie Et Une Nouvelle Musique*, is equipped with charts carefully diagramming this direct lineal descent. As he puts it, his precursors liberated the Word and he pursued their line of thought to its logical conclusion by liberating the Letter.

BEING AND HAVING BEEN

Rauchnitz looked at his typewriter. His typewriter looked at Rauchnitz. Finally, an earwig, crawling out of Sartre's *Nausea*, climbed up and entered his ear. He swivelled his pelvis like Elvis Presley and for a moment went into "double or nothing": had his plane been rerouted for Cuba? Was he in a plane? What was real? What was unreal? Should he talk to his analyst about it? Or had his analyst just broken with his old school and joined a group of fractionary therapists in rebellion against the obsolete teachings of the Old Master? He stopped a minute to watch the Mets game, to see how it was going. Ha, ha, those Americans, he thought.

I can't see anything good coming out of what's being written these days. Some criminal is bound to take advantage of the situation to make trouble for the author. Maybe one day man will rise above the level of monkeys. In the meantime, all I can do is mutter, "Onward, evolution!" Yes, maybe the times are bad. Execrations are springing up everywhere. Those damned execrations! Let poor old Carl Goy praise spirituality, the materialists come down on him. Let him praise materialism, and the spiritualists come down on him. There's nowhere to hide.

Often, a childlike look glows in his eyes and he dreams again. When he was younger, fishing in the stream at Rockaway, watching the cork, waiting for it to disappear under the water. That moment of excitement and intense joy when he got a bite. At three years old, the treachery of grown-ups made him cry, when, without his knowing it, the members of his family hooked a dead fish to his line and pretended that he had caught it. They can never leave nature alone in its marvelous abundance. Always manipulations!

Judging by the tone I've used since the beginning of this book, can't you see me already as another Lautrèamont? You're right. I am another Lautrèamont. It's the only tone I can adopt, old chap, since Lautrèamont used it! Rimbaud always seemed like a matinee idol to me. *And I've never seen myself as a matinee idol.*

No, for me they're just shadows. The shadows of anonymity, or, in literature, the realm of the pseudonym. Avoiding all publicity, I remain the man who appears in a footnote at the bottom of the page, in somebody else's testimony, the man who almost made himself understood, the man who influenced genius—then vanished. It's a particular species, a certain well-defined type. It's someone legendary, never made of flesh and blood. He's never known by his works, but always by the vague awareness of his presence. He stays crouched behind the civil war, chewing a Tootsie Roll. During the riots, he cowered in the lobby. The man in front of him or behind him in the cafeteria committed a murder, or is going to commit one. But as for him, he's a social security number, a blood type, a belly that has to be filled. ALL THIS BECAUSE OF AN INNATE TIMIDITY. In class, when a difficult question was asked that only he knew the answer to, he wouldn't answer because that would put an end to the charade, and he just laughed. Always the mystery man!

I'm going to interrupt my paean to the unknown for a minute, to amuse you with an anecdote concerning the sex life of a well-loved poet. It seems he had always wanted to have an affair with a man, but never knew how to go about it. So, on this occasion, while in Dakar as a sailor in the merchant marine during wartime, he asked around among the local pimps for a sex object. The meeting was arranged, and Ginsberg, trembling with anticipation, met his beloved. It was a hunchbacked dwarf. O tempora, o mores, there's one for the celebrity circuit!

FLY-PAPER THOUGHTS

As a longtime reader of Kafka and even of Sartre (*The Flies*), my relationships with the insect world have been led at different levels. As a young boy, I enjoyed running through the house, a can of insecticide in my hand, killing all the flies. In fact, the other children whom

I knew, and myself, were fascinated and moved in various ways by the insects around us. I remember one kid, whose ambition was to become a doctor, who pulled the wings off a butterfly. Many similar atrocities were committed by the budding scientists of the day, before the atomic bomb. I wonder what they're doing now.

Around 1956, during a strange period when I felt that I was not as ferocious as the norm, a period of madness, I remember once again killing flies against the asylum walls, TO PROVE TO MYSELF THAT I EXISTED.

I seem to have images in my head of restaurants I used to go to in the thirties, of many strips of flypaper, covered in flies, hanging from the ceiling. When we have nothing else to think about, our attention focuses from time to time on the fly, or on some other insect. The reason why insects figure so often in fantastic literature is that it is inevitable for the majority of men to ask themselves how man, the grotesque persecutor, must appear to the insect world. The gulf between the infinitely large and the infinitely small often crops up in Swift, and in other thinkers, and is a subject of constant fascination to the idle.

REPORT FROM THE BRONX

Ubuesque, Beckettlike, or Kafkian? Which is the better adjective? Nonetheless, at the northern limit of the city, the emotional undercurrents are much the same as, say, in the San Remo. We receive daily newscast therapy from Walter Cronkite. Danger seems to grow like compound interest. Liberal, conservative, communist, and fascist conspiracies crop up everywhere and vie for attention. Nobody pays much attention to me anymore. I am no longer described as either a hipnik or a beatster. I fish at City Island where the social issues are forgotten in the quest for flounders and blackfish. All this is comforting, yet disquieting. I realize that I have fled to the farthest limits of serenity afforded by the city. Occasionally, I make it down to the Village and see a little of the other extreme of behavior. Over the whole city lurks a *Marat-Sade* mood, an *Alice in Wonderland* mood, as if a lunatic nightmare has become real.

Obscenity has become the only mode of expression pretty nearly. This is not freedom of speech, it is the triumph of subnormality over sex. What can we expect from social forces? Almost anything. A writer commits suicide almost every day. Burroughs is always leaving for London, Ginsberg is always in California, Kerouac is always in Florida. The literati are always on the move and it is useless to attempt to keep up with them. The only thing to do seems to be to keep gazing sidelong at TV. The TV is more effective than the analyst. I have tried both, and have concluded that what we want is *facts*. Not subjective fantasy or interpersonal gibberish, but the cold hard objective facts that exist apart from psychotic aberration.

VIVE LA DIFFÉRENCE

It must have been difficult for Chinamen and Japanese in Spain during the Civil War. When a Japanese said he was for the "Royalists" he was thought to be for the extreme right. When a Chinaman said he was for the "Loyalists," he was thought to be for the extreme left.

Note: As you know, Japanese pronounce "*l*" as "*r*" and Chinese pronounce "*r*" as "*l*".

PROBLEMS

Two of the most important problems facing us today are those of Mental Stealth and Excremental Health.

BON MOT

If you lose contact with the Zeitgeist, never fear. You may still have contact with the poltergeist.

ON THE ONE HAND AND
ON THE OTHER

A man's philosophy dies with him, brother. You can't carry those paperbacked founts of knowledge with you into the grave. Why not die babbling of starfish?

MY REACTION TO SEXUAL
AND OTHER ABERRATIONS

As one becomes accustomed to living among the various multifoliate aspects of the sexual revolution (a word justifying any number of sexual practices) one becomes accustomed to them and less disturbed by deviations from the ordinary. Also one becomes less likely to experiment for experiment's sake.

ARMAND LE FOU

"*Corsaire aux cheveux d'or!*", Odette shrieked while I read from the Lautréamont I had stolen from the surrealist exposition. Suddenly, a shot rang out and everybody ducked. "*C'est Armand le Fou!*" she cried pointing at a slim dark-haired man with a revolver in his hand, *un trés mauvais garçon*.

UNDERGROUND DIARY—1967

No parades today. At last a day without a parade. For peace, for war, it makes little difference to me. I'm staying in today, waiting for a call from an agency about a job. Time on one's hands before the Met game begins at 2:00. So I may as well write. Sometimes these jottings can be traded for bread. Somebody or other interested in the travail of an intelligent man. And I am an intelligent man. I took a test and my IQ is slightly above average so my experiences have something of the common denominator about them.

Amid all the charivari about war and peace there does seem to be a cultural renaissance going on. My girlfriend and I saw *Ulysses* the other day and it was a memorable film. Everything I recalled from the book was there. There is more than utter blankness if one goes out and seeks it. In the great works of art there is a palliative, a palliative for the deadly tedium of existence. A tedium for which I blame no one—not McNamara, not Ho Chi Minh, not the psychiatrists (God bless them) but for which one can only blame the blood in one's veins, the veins that keep throbbing in physical splendor in the face of intellectual frustration and dissatisfaction.

The war charivari sometimes makes me think back to all the wars during which I have been alive. The Italians versus the Ethiopians, the Russians versus the Finns, the Chinese versus the Japanese, the Albanians versus the Italians, the Italians versus the Greeks, the Germans versus the French, et cetera, et cetera into modern times.

Wars always elicit poems attributing to them idealistic purposes or glory of one sort or another. In this war opinion seems bitterly divided and I can't get worked up over the virtues of either side. In any case, I am apparently useless to both groups of antagonists. Neither finds me a worthwhile ally in these cases. I have proved my unworthiness to both. I am completely unreliable and tend to believe they are both mad. In any case, I have won my right to be aloof. The Marxists seem to me to be bent upon farts and violence. The other side also makes absurd demands on one's credibility. There are repellent things that both sides seem to be bent on cramming down the throats of the free man. Both sides talk in terms of their official cliches. I am neither especially religious nor am I a Marxist. I don't want to mouth the cliches of either side because both seem false. The Bertrand Russell business in Sweden only calls to mind the hypocrisy of the lefties in time past, an hypocrisy of which I am only too well aware. And the righties who they are protesting against have their obvious hypocrisies. Why not accept the charges that both hurl at each other as being absolutely true. They mutually expose the crimes of each other.

The charivari will go on indefinitely with no hero and no vanquished. Yesterday's victors are today's vanquished. This makes me recall a poem called "Ozymandias" about the fleeting glory of a "King of Kings." As Artaud said, there is nothing to do but to pile up the bodies, gloriously or ingloriously dead. This is the bitter irony of life as Shakespeare pointed out in the Gravedigger's scene in *Hamlet*. After all, it is only a gigantic show we are putting on.

Well, at the moment the Marxists seem to be the repellent ones, with their lies about peace and democracy. I have forgotten the unfriendliness of the right, by this I mean the ones who refused to accept me as a non-Marxist ally and friend, though I intellectually sided with them. But in wars I suppose there is hypersuspicion on both sides.

CÉLINE, ARTAUD, GENET

These writers fit certain moods that one may fall into at certain times. Céline I discovered at 19 after reading about him in the work of Henry Miller. For a while I was considerably impressed by him, later began to measure his defects against his assets. I do not worship Céline, though I have read him. Artaud's picture and voice resemble his prose and I have found him interesting from time to time. Genet falls into the same category and when I first read *Pompes Funèbres* in the forties I was deeply affected by it. However, none of these writers trespass on new ground. There were others in their respective realms before them and after them, others who crowd out their memory for me. And too much expertise or analysis removes the thrill of the original reading. I do not accept the concept of a literary vanguard or elite adopting a heroic pose. Anyone may trespass on their sacred territory. Ditto Sartre who once said that philosophy is for specialists. Everybody is a philosopher. Though, I will add that when I read Genet, I acquired a *stealthier* attitude toward life.

PEOPLE OF THE FIFTIES AND SIXTIES

Wild, crazy bouncing around. "Dig everything," says Kerouac. They are reading *The Book of Changes*. What changes can possibly occur after those I have already known, I wonder. William Carlos Williams' letter comes to Pilgrim State hospital, "Life is not over in a day." This seems bullshit to me. My life is over. Much squawking, much yawking. Apparently it's not over. Doctors, doctors, patients, patients. Letters from poets, writing to poets. Confused conglomeration of visitors from various phases of my life. Confused rehabilitation courses, this, that, reading at the Metro, meeting B.H. He is rehabilitated. He helped me when I escaped. World collapsing a dozen times over and being rebuilt. Babies born, deaths in the family. *Philosophy of a Lunatic: Wit, Wisdom, And Folly* bought at the Gotham Book Mart. For three dollars or so and change. Take it seriously and you have entrance to the bliss and sorrow of the mentally ill. Don't go there anymore. No more dangerous esoterica. This reading thing can be extremely bad. Read a story in newspaper recently about a boy in the west who bought and read Camus' *L'Etranger*, then shot somebody. Hadn't Leopold and Loeb been reading Nietzsche? How many crimes have been indirectly caused by writers unknown to the reader? Wasn't Oswald reading *The Militant*? Wasn't the man arrested for attempting to blow up the Russian Embassy probably a reader of some right-wing paper? The pen is mightier than the sword. More often than not it directs the sword. Writing entails grave responsibilities. Read the *Times* and avoid folly. Read the *Post* and meet a nice, Jewish girl looking for a husband. Read the *News* and go out to the ballpark or go fishing. Read the *Daily Worker* and go underground. Read the *Enquirer* for laughs. Read the *East Village Other* and be hip and psychedelic. Read braille and speak hesitantly but correctly. Read *War and Peace* and enter another era. Read the *Geographic* and bask under a tropical sun. Read Proust when you are in jail and have plenty of time. What are you reading lately? This question probes exactly into one's present frame of mind. The book makes the mood and the mood makes the book. Libraries win or lose elections. Does it help the identity problem to realize that the same man may read *Candy* one week and the Bible the next, and may be the one type of reader the one week and the other the next? What about *My Secret Life* by Mao Tse-tung?

THOUGHTS ON MARIJUANA, RELIGIOUS EXPERIENCE, AND THE SUPERNATURAL

At times the above factors have occupied my attention, but experience has taught me to shun these issues in conversation and above all to respect other people's difference of opinion with me on these issues. No one has the final say. Also subterfuge, lying, ulterior motive, and hypocrisy play large roles where such issues are concerned. In a nexus so complicated it seems wisest to me to withhold all final judgments and to wait and see. Until death and the existence or non-existence of the hereafter. Among religious reading which played some part in my life have been Kierkegaard, St. John of the Cross, Eliot, Bloy, Maritain, Thomas Merton, Christopher Smart, Dante, Blake, Charles Peguy, and Kafka. Also a bit of Zen for a while, and at an early age the transcendentalist thought of Emerson and Whitman. Carried to extremes these interests seem to cause as much or more public annoyance and consternation than the highly taboo atheistic doctrines of Marx, Baudelaire, or Artaud or the diabolism of Huysmans or de Sade. The annoying thing is that whichever position you take, religious or anti-religious for argument's sake (and life I firmly believe is merely conducted for argument's sake) there will always be someone beside you who condemns you as *lache* or degenerate from the point of view of either Leninism or Algerian nationalism or God knows what else.

Marijuana, for example. For some it is a religious act to smoke pot. For others, it is an irreligious act (just another high for reasons of self-indulgence and sensual stimulation, like alcohol but less sloppy). My position here (among the many I could take with equal comfort) is that its illegality makes it a nuisance at the present time with tea-head fanatics demanding of company and confraternity all over the place acting hurt if you simply don't care to get into trouble.

Striking and admirable as some martyrs of reason or unreason may be, like Nietzsche, Joan of Arc, or Marat or the multitude of martyr types of the present day both of left and right, their uncompromising quality interferes with my most prized possession, simply *joie de vivre*, or, less fancy, comfort. Live as you wish. As for me, I'm making it now, I'm not complaining. Join me if you possibly can.

MY CHANGING VIEW OF FRANCE

My earliest picture of France and of Frenchmen was one of men with finely waxed mustaches and round hats with visors who spoke through their noses and were always saying things like "Vive La Fwance!" They also said things like "Ils ne passeront pas," guarded the Maginot line, detested the Boche, and always sang songs like "La Marseillaise" and "Frère Jacques." They always seemed slightly effete but were very gallant.

For a long period, this image of France disappeared and was replaced by that of Resistance fighters wearing raincoats and furtively sneaking up and down alleyways. This soon blended into the picture of the French existential tough, cigarette sticking miraculously to his lips in all hectic situations, who shrugged, always shrugged, when anything tragic, hair-raising, or heart-rending occurred.

This touched off a period of expatriatism in me when I actually went to France and picked up a million and one intimate details of actual French life to fill out the picture. My accent changed, I knew some current argot, popular songs, current poets and painters, the names of existent streets and cafés. This became somewhat watered-down and became a peculiar blend of French and Jewish mannerisms when my expatriatism became limited to the fifties Greenwich Village scene. From expatriate to Fran-cophile during that also brief period.

Eventually, though, Greenwich Village became cut off to me also, and my scene changed into the original American Jewish scene now free of the fifties-ish exis-tentialist elixir. The Jewish Shrug replaced the French Shrug. And, lo and behold, I began to think of French-men as wearing thin mustaches again and always coming out with "Vive La Fwance!" I stopped reading Prévert, Queneau, Michaux, and *Les Temps Modernes* and settled for what I could get in my neighborhood public library. I began reading Victor Hugo, Dumas, Balzac, etc. Again, as in childhood, I began thinking of French as "a beau-tiful language." Adieu Rimbaud, Céline, Genet, Bau-delaire, de Sade and ship ahoy our NATO allies. I maintain that this is now the only viable view of France for me. A Frog is a Frog is a Frog. Any other attitude would, in the resurrected native philistinism, mark me as a "weirdo."

APROPOS THE TAJ MAHAL

Nobody at all mentions the Taj Mahal these days. Yet it was one of the great romantic dreams of my child-hood to see the Taj Mahal. Some iconoclast might even shatter convention by jumping into and swimming around in its pool. Richard Halliburton in, I believe, *The Royal Road to Romance* (or was it *The Flying Carpet?*) had a shimmering photograph of the glistening dome in one of the high points of his very popular travel and adventure book. My father, an avid reader, often mentioned this fabulous tomb built by a great emperor for his deceased wife. And it was a dream of my childhood someday to see the Taj Mahal. But the romantic dreams of one decade are, alas, not the romantic dreams of a decade forty years removed. My poet-friend Allen went to India in the early sixties, and I even drank champagne with him, Peter Orlovsky, Louis Ginsberg, LeRoi Jones (Amiri Baraka), and some other people in his cabin on the *America* just before sailing time. And Allen never once (as I recall) mentioned the Taj Mahal in his writing about India. One of my female cousins married a young Pakistani in the seventies and took a trip (well, to Pakistan not India) with him and was never under the spell I am probably still under—the idea of the Taj Mahal as being one of the wonders of the world. For that matter who ever speaks these days of the wonders of the earth? Maybe Allen Ginsberg himself is one of the present-day wonders of the earth. During World War II, many Americans served in the China-India-Burma theater, and I suppose many of them may have been under the old spell and did visit the glistening dome, etc. They were probably the last. When I was a seaman some ships I might have caught went to Karachi and might have set in motion such an adventure for me, but other forces were in motion in my mind just then and the lure of the Occidental *caveaux* of Saint-Germain-des-Prés held a greater attraction for me. Sensibility had even by then so changed.

It is very likely technology which brings about these decade by decade changes in one's fantasy life. There was a day when Lautréamont could get a rise out of me with Maldoror's sexual adventures with female sharks. This seemed superreal at that time. Yet fairly recently

I glimmed some flicks showing women making it with horses and pigs and dogs, and at that moment Lautréamont seemed, fateful word, to have been *absorbed*. As Artaud had been absorbed and the Taj Mahal has long ago been absorbed.

Searching for a new *frisson* to keep my mind from withering away and to keep the old excitement still alive, I try desperately to hitch myself to this magical technology which plays so alchemically with men's minds. I learned to operate a computerized cash register and experienced something of a Marinetti-like thrill at this futurism-of-the-seventies. I, simple me, touch the button, and it connects with an enormous Rube Goldberg machine somewhere computing enormous records. Marinetti was the poet of fast cars circa 1920 and was the prophet of Neal Cassady and of Marlon Brando's popularity. He eventually was killed fighting against the Soviet Union on the Eastern front in World War II. There was a conflict even then among those seminal poets and thinkers of the early century centering around technology, the then new technology. Some, like Marinetti, felt that the speed, the *élan*, was the revolutionary thing, the motif of change. Others, socialists of that day, felt that the social and economic changes brought about by the technology would touch off the really important revolution. Cocteau's famous Nazi-like motorcyclists with their homosexual et cetera on the one hand and treatises on what the production of motorcycles et cetera would do to the relations between capital and labor (this as the Hegelian-Marxian crux) on the other hand.

I feel this conflict of ideas about motivation for the new technology as I press, button by button, the keys of my magical computer register. My labor, the cost of my labor, the final product, surplus value milked from my labor, et cetera, et cetera.

Marinetti died on the Russian front, on that cold damned Russian front. And we all know what Marinetti finally stood for. Where were his fast cars then? Where were Cocteau's Nazi-like motorcyclists? And Rommel's dashing turned-up hat?

Which should bring us back to talk, nostalgic, et cetera from a balding man about childish dreams, encouraged by his father, about the Taj Mahal—still a glistening monument to an emperor's deceased wife—but now ignored by glamorizers everywhere.

WAR

War comes like a zephyr and leaves like one. Before you know it, the armies have marched to the strategic point and it is over. Something has changed. You never know where you were at the key points. It is always lived in retrospect. Years later, it is discussed and argued about and people reminisce. The reminiscences become confused and the voices rise as past accusations of cowardice and boasts of men proclaiming their heroism are heard. You buy the map. The map has changed. The boundary lines are different. Screams of REVANCH-ISME and cheating are heard. The bars reverberate with boasts. Uniforms are seen then discarded. The "new world" and the "post-war" motif again become evident. First the heroic generation, then the cynical Lost Generation, sitting around emotionally castrated like Jake Barnes and friends. Soon we will be coining names for the post-Vietnam generation. Their humor, their aspirations. History repeats. It always repeats. It repeats eternally. And so, having lived through it before I recognize it. The conflict over war aims. "MAKE SURE THE WAR IS A MORAL WAR." Again the USO, the objectors, the objectors camps, and Norman Thomas. This is where I came in.

HO HUM

What did you say? Oh, I thought so. The trouble with writing is that it conjures up mock excitement over things that would better be yawned at. Does the state of the world ever deserve anything more than to be yawned at? Very well. Conjure up mock excitement if you like. Tell me that such and such coup d'etat or nuclear blast deserves at least a raised eyebrow. Or a sex orgy in protest. Or a new dance. I'll go along with you for a little while and then I'll lose interest. Not to offend you, of course, but simply because I have already moved on to the next subject of interest—a bizarre new commercial advertising a bizarre new lemonade. Or perhaps I have leaped back in time to remember a midget auto race of the 1930s or moved up in time to imagine what it would be like to live to 200. "The last time I saw him, he was a Buddhist. Now he has raised a mustache." There seems to be no thought-policeman to limit these imaginings. That is the trouble. I can go anywhere I want in thought. This can also eliminate automobiles. A very charming dream, I think, would be an interview with the Count of Lautreàmont and a discussion with him over two cups of black coffee (he has come back to life) of *The Songs Of Maldoror*. Or a discussion of the issues of life and death with Jacques Rigaut the evening prior to his suicide. Or a discussion of the issues of the Void with Antonin Artaud over pizza on Bleecker Street. Ho Hum.

CONFESSIONS OF A CREEP

You really have no idea how left out of it all I feel. All the hullabaloo and nowhere am I fully appreciated. Appreciate me! "We all want to be appreciated," says some goddamned psychologist. Trying to include me in the "all." But he doesn't understand anymore than anyone has ever understood. I want to be appreciated in some perverse, incongruous fashion that *definitely* excludes me from that glowing, once prodigal, now loved group he alludes to that wants to be appreciated in perhaps the normal, mundane fashion. Those who do not insist upon their separateness.

Nothing infuriates me like the word "in." Don't you want to be one of the "in" group? Go to the "in" places and all that hocus pocus. Look now, one has either always been "in" or been "out." And I have always been "out!" All the grinning in the world and all the rubbing of chins in hermetic fashion won't get us anywhere, any more than it has in the last thirty-nine years. I warn you!

You are all a bunch of finks in the metaphysical or theological sense even more than you are in the secular sense. You are *cosmic* finks! Hurray for me! Long live me! Hurray, hurray!

"We love you," say no end of saccharine letters to me while I lie on my cot of the damned. Do you know how I distrust the word "love?" If you had written that you hated me I would feel that I was getting more just recognition. You hand me a peppermint candy. What the hell am I going to do with this? If you had tried to poison me I would have felt more ennobled.

* * *

Well, perhaps I am just cryptic—a bundle of contradictions. Just like you. But wait, just wait, until I get the upper hand.

THE ART VACUUM

My oh my! We are now asking one another to write each other letters so we can sell them to museums as the work of great poets, seers, or what have you. The truth is that we are merely people wearing horn-rimmed glasses with nothing to do but read the *New York Times Book Review* on Sunday and see our images reflected in the types in the *New Yorker* cartoons. Since lettrism, I feel that I am making a contribution to the surging forward development of poetry by merely plunging my spoon into a plate of alphabet soup.

I promise to try harder. Maybe someday I'll think of something to say that is not a prelude to a mildly dyspeptic belch.

The space flights leave a gigantic "Ho hum!" Even the Void, that non-existent place where poets once went when they really wanted Out, has been consumed a thousand times over by the cannibal art-public. What can survive the appetite of the ravenous human race to consume every drop of juice from every natural fruit, existing in the time-hypothesis we inhabit, before it vanishes. Before it vanishes? It has always droolingly (disgusted by its own drool) pleaded the imminence of extinction. Oh, cowardly, clever, conniving animal. So you're afraid of The Bomb? You bore me to death! And only yesterday you were pleading world-weariness and seeking an Out. Only to come back today, mascara your eyelids and prepare for another debauch in the form of a "Ban the Bomb" pageant.

THE GAME BETWEEN MANHATTAN STATE AND PILGRIM STATE

(Sometime in the Early Sixties)

Rather than write about the immediate present and precipitate lawsuits and protests and acts of revenge from persons who I would write about in present circumstances and who may feel that I am treating them unfairly, I will write about persons long forgotten and events long forgotten and passed into nothingness. The game I am writing about occurred during the second of my three incarcerations in Pilgrim State Hospital in West Brentwood, Long Island. It occurred, historically, sometime between the Cuban Missile Crisis and the assassination of John F. Kennedy. The only connection between this era described and matters "Irish" lies in the fact that Kennedy was President and I myself approved of having a non-Protestant chief executive since I felt it was evidence of democracy at work.

Anyway, the hospital contained one baseball fanatic named Danny Parrish and little Danny was of course the sparkplug of the sports-mindedness that broke out among us patients on the occasion of a game between Manhattan State and Pilgrim State. Pilgrim wore bright red uniforms and Manhattan wore white uniforms similar to the Mets. Pilgrim players were ethnically different also, consisting mainly of tall, gangling blacks, while Manhattan's players were mostly short and somewhat maimed Puerto Ricans (or Hispanics, as they are now called). One of Manhattan's outfielders, I remember, had one arm.

Manhattan State did not bring along a cheering section of lunatics (partially cured I should state, since they were capable of partisan preferences) so we Pilgrim State rooters were enormously gratified to find the game, almost from the first pitch, becoming a ridiculous slaughter. Manhattan's one-armed outfielder practically went crazy (so to speak) trying to corral the Pilgrimaires' soaring and caroming drives into the outfield. And the result was a 23–2 Pilgrim State victory. I would suggest as a moral to the tale: *The baseball teams of competing lunatic asylums ought to be better matched.*

THE GAME

1975! All aboard for New Haven! Carefully we had planned the trip for a couple of months in advance. I had never seen a college football game in all my 47 years. And I had a sort of surly underdog complex. I'd been put down, but badly, by American society, and had never done the things I would have liked to have done with my life. I felt double-crossed, as though society had never made good on the promises it had made to me in my earliest years. All of a sudden, up pops this cousin of mine, a Yalie, with an offer to get me a ticket to the Yale-Harvard game—The Game—in this year of 1975. Everybody on the damned train was headed for The Game. All kinds of very stylish-looking blond guys, some of them with raccoon-skin coats in imitation of the twenties Scott Fitzgerald era. Nobody plebian here you could be damned sure. Anyway I make it out to New Haven and there is my cuz right on the button with a bag full of sandwiches he made for us to eat at the game. He is less than half my age but already something of a gourmet. We make it out to the Bowl, which is the real-life replica of the diagrams I'd seen of it in football schedules. Long, with rounded ends. The tickets my cuz got were for the student section. We filed into that area. Gee whiz! Those college people looked like children to me. How time flies! The Yale team came out, the Harvard team came out. When the Harvard team came out, the Yale students rose as one and chanted the following: "Borrr-ing—Inconsequential." In my mind, I compared this sort of behavior with the city-type booing and cheering at Shea Stadium.

The game began and it was great. Like watching a live chess game. The big man for Harvard was this cat Kubacki who was also supposed to be a very bright history scholar. I thought of Frank Merriwell and Clint Frank and Albee Booth and Ducky Pond. Yale fought hard, with their star, Don Gesicki. But Harvard won out and won the Ivy League crown for 1975. I came back feeling like—Hell!—like I'd seen the Yale-Harvard game!

AND WHAT OF THE PRESENT?

Ginsberg went to Kerouac's grave in Lowell with Bob Dylan. Last summer, up at Cherry Valley, a girl in her twenties asked me if it were true that Neal Cassady's ashes are strewn in the vicinity. What happened to us all? Remember the intense literary interest, the bitter rivalries, the gossip, the parties? A couple of years ago David Burnett died in a bar from drinking Mason Hoffenberg's methodone dose. And I stopped writing altogether. I became a bookseller and am still tranquilized. Claude is wrong to see tranquilizers as a punishment inflicted on one or as a castration of one's rebelliousness. I refer him to Mark Vonnegut's book on schizophrenia called *The Eden Express*. Tranquilizers are supposed to be the only treatment devised in the mental health field in the last 25 years and Vonnegut points out that they are the un-romantic present-day solution to what he feels to be a strictly bio-chemical (not a philosophical, political, or literary) problem. He writes from personal experience, as I do. Where does this leave, say, Artaud's Van Gogh essay and where does it leave all the surrealist writing on "madness?" It leaves them in the pre-tranquilizer era of mental health history. If anxieties are reduced by tranquilizers, what possible interest can I have in such antediluvian writers? I feel no anxiety, the world seems perfectly real to me—so how can I empathize with your Kafkian protagonist or other existential heroes? And if tranquilizers make one calm, what need have I of Marx? I don't get angry because I feel good. I realize that most of the world's population are not on tranquilizers and that most people are still furiously wielding the old intellectual weapons. Not I.

BADINAGE FOR CLAUDE PELIEU

I sit at my writing desk in the Bronx, where I sat twelve years ago writing the two *Mishaps* books. Traffic roaring by outside? Yes, traffic still roaring by. A bit about the American scene as I've been seeing it during these years? For a literary person, the most striking thing is the virtual omnipresence of pornography. Among the things I've seen on film are a young woman being screwed by a big, fat pig (a real zoological pig) and a female child (about nine) sucking off a bearded grandfatherly-looking old man. The other porn things I've seen are, I suppose, too humdrum to catalogue, though to one of my age, brought up on Mickey Mouse, a little startling to behold on film.

Another thing one is made well aware of, in the course of one's business career, is the atrocious spelling of both young and old—and the appalling paucity of their general knowledge. Only the other day, an attractive young woman approached me in my role as bookseller and asked for a copy of "Lady Bowery." Only after some interrogation did I deduce that she was looking for a copy of *Madame Bovary*. All the above, both the porn and the illiteracy (in this "superpower") are accepted unblinkingly as "normal" at the present time. Dante-esque?

A man came into our book area of the department store wearing a full flesh-colored face mask, beneath which a black beard flowed. He was wearing two pairs of glasses. I quickly walked over to him, sensing something out of line. "Can I help you?" "Do you have anything by Trotsky?" "No, but we do have two new books on Russia." Et cetera, et cetera—during which he claimed to have been a friend of Bernard Kalb and to have been to Russia with him. He left, I was told, cursing. "A mental case," said a bystander.

Another tragic thing that occurred on the New York bohemian scene in recent years was the untimely death of young David Burnett, the anthologist who had, with Eric Protter, been co-editor of *New-Story* magazine in post-World War II Paris. He had somehow permitted himself to drink up, as I heard the story from Stanley Gould, *Candy*-author Mason Hoffenberg's allotted dose of methadone. I was told that he died on the spot in the bar where the incident occurred.

One reads, in the *Times* book page, of "a dwindling national superego" and it rings extremely true in this melange, to me—an ordinary pedestrian, of *opera bouffe* and high tragedy. (Is my limited French plebian in this period of ultra-sophisticated madness?)

OBSERVATION OF POVERTY IN NYC

by Eli Democritus

A big business now—not a big business—but a little business involving many little, very little people (little not in physical dimension, but little in worldly importance) is the business of gathering soda cans from ashcans throughout our great city and selling said cans to local supermarkets. To be eligible for this commerce, the particular can in question is required to be stamped 5 CENTS. The can-gatherer goes his merry way from ashcan to ashcan filling large plastic sacks with these cans. Their work is quiet but efficient. I would estimate, based on my own street peregrinations, that there are at least 5000 people engaged in this minor industry in the Bronx and Manhattan. Once in fact I observed a former fellow-employee at a now defunct local department store engaged in this work (for him at present, a sideline).

As a further observation of poverty, though of a somewhat different nature, is this personal anecdote of sexual "business" recounted to me by a lady of my acquaintance. She is in the habit of cadging small gratuities from me. The particular incident I refer to occurred while she was wending her way one weekday along one of those spacious and beautiful Bronx causeways. A truck stopped, the driver exposed his erect penis to her and he offered her three dollars for a handjob. According to her testimony, she obliged.

I myself have often been the victim of pickpocketing and hat stealing on public conveyances—to such a degree in fact that I have now been compelled to use express buses for interboro travel, buses which I can ill afford with my present salary as a Manhattan messenger.

I am acquainted too with many people in Manhattan

who spend every night sleeping in some doorway or other. There are countless people with whom I am not individually acquainted who inhabit nearly all the benches along Central Park on Fifth Avenue with their bags and bedding every night.

HASSELS AND PIPE DREAMS

Back in my thirties I cherished the pipe dream of becoming a department store Santa Claus when I reached my sixties. I am nearly there now chronologically and the Christmas season is approaching. Yet I can only sense the intense disapproval I would meet from the Jewish congregation whose meetings I have been attending. I sense, too, the disapproval I would meet from friends and what remains of family. So another benevolent idea must be discarded to make way for snobbism and ancient hatreds. I had envisaged a cheerful and contented old age. Another carrot of delusion used to make bunny-me race faster during my thirties. Now that old age comes close, hoary horrors emerge from the murk of the centuries to becloud even that golden state. Arguments over tombstones. Shit, man, dig that—*arguments over tombstones!*

OH, YOU FALSE APOCALYPSE

It's been nearly twenty years since I first heard speak of you.

Twenty years ago, poets began speaking about you, and the teenagers swooned.

"It's the end. Live for the moment. Love. Love. Love."

I know that what I say isn't popular, because there are no orgies in it, nor seven-scoop chocolate ice cream cones.

But at the risk of bringing you down, allow me to state that I do not believe we are on the brink of apocalypse, or for twenty years to come.

My longjohns are in the dresser, awaiting another winter; there's still enough mouthwash in the bathroom cabinet.

And next year's carrot harvest will be a good one.

Sleep well and I'll see you in the morning.

VI
BEAT
REFLECTIONS

AN EXHILARATING PROFESSION

I

became a writer very early in life but achieved no degree of recognition until my twenties when I became affiliated with a group of young men who thought I was very talented. My talents lasted five years until they told me that I was no longer talented. I went mad with disappointment. However through my madness my talents reached full bloom and I can now speak to you again.

Rock 'n' Roll.

This dance or music reached full prominence at one point in my illness.

I

experienced *nothing* of it except as a peripheral activity that was going on while I was trying to recontact my "friends."

Stavrogin—several years ago, early in my career, there were a number of people who thought themselves to be this character from one of Dostoyevski's novels—they no longer think so and have forgotten they have ever read Dostoyevski, if they ever really had.

Tranquilizers seem to me to be the best solution for sleepless nights. As well as for the other problems of nervousness and despair. One must learn to take it easy.

A NOTE ON THE REAL
ALLEN GINSBERG

I feel this clown before your eyes is merely a double. The real Allen Ginsberg ... *Le Grand Allen Ginsberg* ... had been raised on Madagascar and spoke only Malagache. I remember his always wearing knickers. The man before your eyes we shall refer to hereafter as *Le Petit Allen Ginsberg*. Yes, I remember clearly now, in the early days of the beatnik generation when we first formed the conception of the marvelous poetic renaissance that followed, living in Chinese restaurants and harassed by the police ... he wore knickers and I wore leotards.

To the future, to the past, and to all the days in between I dedicate the reading of these literary documents.

FOR JACK KEROUAC

Some years ago, I yearned for pancakes in a place where there wasn't even toilet paper.

I complained about this fact to Jack Kerouac, by mail.

I received a letter in reply telling me about a new brand of pancake mix known, coincidently, as "Hungry Jack."

He wasn't spoofing me because I have now seen TV commercials advertising just this brand, "Hungry Jack."

I should now like to take a moment to praise this man for honesty and sharp powers of observation.

ANOTHER DAY, ANOTHER DOLLAR . . . AFTER THE BEAT GENERATION

The New York Mets symbolize for me the spirit of the sixties.

They are the latter-day beatniks of baseball.

In the fifties we had Spillane, now we have Ian Fleming. Which is gorier, I can't say.

Is Genet still a jailbird?

Civil Rights demonstrations have superceded Bird Parker and Dizzy Gillespie in Negro folklore.

Psychoanalysis is good for some people, not for me. I prefer tranquilizers.

Never having mastered the mambo, I am now baffled by the twist and the frug.

My idea of the perfect portrait of Apollinaire would be an apple poised in mid-air.

Most of the poets I meet nowadays are trade school graduates.

One of Allen Ginsberg's first comments about me was, "Large reading, I suppose."

What followed was a description of Burroughs, Kerouac, Huncke, several others.

Yes, in mental hospitals patients still dance and dream hazily about the nurses.

Others discuss anything from Artaud to Schweitzer and Oleg Cassini and some still wave their rumps.

Dirty words create a feeling of surprise in one, that is all.

Obscenity soon becomes boring.

SUGGESTIONS TO IMPROVE THE PUBLIC IMAGE OF THE BEATNIK

It is most important now to change the smell of the beatnik. Instead of using, for example, the word "shit" so often in their poems, I suggest that they tactfully substitute the word "roses" wherever the other word occurs.

This is a small adjustment.

It is just as *avant-garde* so art will suffer no loss.

Instead of saying *"merde"* they will be saying "A rose is a rose is a rose is a rose." Just as *avant-garde*, you see, with considerable improvement in the effect created.

WILLIAM BURROUGHS—AS I LEARNED OF HIM

I have never been a "disciple" of Burroughs (always having been afraid of drugs and anything associated with it) and my knowledge of him is fragmentary. His appeal to me has been in his genius as a prose writer (I liked *Junky*, the best of his books; but his world is always interesting). He is an expert at pinpointing types in modern society and seems familiar with these types on all levels of the social and anti-social register. He is an expert on the plagues of the cities, the conning, the cheating, the boasting, the false glory. And the vanity and self-deceit of people on all levels.

I learned of him this way. Ginsberg described him in 1950 as an as-yet-undiscovered genius living in Mexico

City with a wife and children. He was not a writer as yet but might one day blossom forth. As it happened, I had an uncle in publishing at that time and later in the course of that year, Ginsberg persuaded Burroughs, as he had persuaded me earlier, to try to put some of his insights onto paper. We dreamed up the idea of a book for him to write: *Junk*, the story of a habit. Chapter by chapter this came through and working on it, revising it, recommending changes, was a really exciting editorial experience.

Burroughs still didn't want to be known as the book's author and used the pseudonym, William Lee. With each revised portion came a note to Allen signed: Willie Lee, your junkie writing-boy.

FOREWORD TO JUNKY

Junky by William Seward Burroughs was originally entitled *Junk* and was written under the pseudonym of William Lee. First presented for publication in the early fifties, it aroused some interest among hardcover publishers but was brought out as one of the earliest paperbacks of the newly emerging Ace Books.

Since that time, Burroughs has become famous here and abroad as an avant-garde novelist and short story writer, writing under his own name. His novel *Naked Lunch* has been brought out by City Lights. *The Soft Machine* and *The Ticket That Exploded* have been published in Paris by Olympia Press with much attendant scandal. And a new novel *Nova Express*, will soon be brought out by Grove.

In Norman Mailer's *Advertisements For Myself*, Burroughs is referred to as the American Jean Genet. His second novel, *Queer*, remains unpublished in this country and abroad.

Behind the "beat" renaissance in mid-20th century America, which shocked the sensibilities of some and gave new expression to others, William Burroughs remains a seldom seen but by now legendary figure. In 1964, unlike 1950, he has innumerable imitators and would-be imitators. His early creed of junk as a way of life has seeped into the youth of today to the point of becoming a major national problem.

In *Junky* he is factual. This is his earlier mode. In his more recent work, he ventures into the surrealistic and imaginative. The New York *Post*, in writing of his subject matter, fantasies (homoerotic), and experiments in technique, finds him verging sometimes on the infantile and the schizoid.

In life, he is a peculiar kind of adventurer, seeking out what is unusual or unexplored in our sensibilities or in our way of living. Pursuing what is increasingly hard to find, the unknown, Burroughs has not yet become redundant and his curiosity is not yet exhausted. In this respect he is unlike many other so-called avant-gardists and poets who once experimented but then reclined on their couches and ruefully admitted that there was nothing new under the sun.

As for his junk habit, he has gone off and gone back on and taken a variety of cures with different amounts of success. One cure, in England, under a Dr. Dent, resulted in an article written by Burroughs in a scientific quarterly.

Burroughs is a Harvard graduate, has pursued a variety of occupations, is the father of two children, and is the scion of a wealthy family.

One of the more lurid incidents in his past was the accidental shooting of his wife in a "William Tell" experiment . . . demonstrating his marksmanship by attempting to shoot a champagne glass off her head and killing her in the process. For this, in Mexico City, in about 1950, he was acquitted.

In one form or another, under one guise or another, his character and personality seem to have had reflections in fictional characters in the writings of his protégé, Jack Kerouac. This is particularly evident in the character of Dennison in Kerouac's first novel, *The Town and the City*, and also in that of Bull Balloon in *Dr. Sax*.

His politics are a bit hazy. We can seldom make out whether he is fighting against real conspiracies or imaginary ones. In *In Search of Yage*, he appears at times to be a liberal or even a radical, and the reputation he acquired in recent years in Paris seems to situate him more or less on the left. Most of the time, Burroughs appears to be too self-preoccupied to show much sustained interest in any political camp.

PSYCHIATRIC INSTITUTE

We waited on that horrible ward. Amid talk of Hampton and Gillespie, we thought we would be beaten to death or ostracized. In full view of the audience we thought of hell.

Ginsberg for his crimes and I for my mummery. Hair, dandruff, decadent fertility.

He began talks on Holmes, Cannastra, Kerouac, Lucien, Burroughs, others began speaking of stigmata of the damned. I spoke of Nijinsky, the Marines at Vladivostok and Fanny Hurst.

Terror, excruciating terror.

ALLEN AT PI

Yeats and Spengler were much on his mind. Read me Yeats' "The Second Coming" ("the falcon no longer hears the falconer"). Some discussion of Toynbee, just published in the U.S. Neal Cassady represents the "internal proletariat" of Toynbee—the hope of the West. The West not the East represents the future. I like the franks and beans at the Silver Palms. Irving Rottman digs his cream puffs. Aaron Fromm talks to people only after receiving a visit. Sam Weinstein is worried about three pimples on his cock. Nathan Grossman thinks, at times, that he is Gerhard Eisler. Ginsberg has painted a striking Golgotha in the OT shop. He calls the nurses "Nursey-wursey." Kerouac comes on a visit. Ginsberg tells me that this guy is going to be the novelist of the future.

THE SHROUDED STRANGER OF THE NIGHT

For any Ginsberg scholars interested in Allen's early ideas, let me say that I enjoyed exposure to the early Ginsberg and became acquainted with one of the ideas that haunted and fascinated him during, I imagine, *The Empty Mirror* period. This was the vision, or concept, of a sort of mysterious necromancer, both ugly and beautiful, who haunted River Street, in Paterson, and laughed to himself and cast spells world-wide in scope. Far removed from the adult big-wheel Ginsberg so into politics, the necromancer, a product of a youthful fanciful mind, was referred to as "the Shrouded Stranger of the Night." Allen and Kerouac had this poetic mythology in common and in the character of the Shrouded Stranger lay the embryo of Kerouac's Dr. Sax.

POETRY READING

Alfred Goonsberg, Lothario Furso, Pietro Orloff, a woman writer of a somewhat yellowish hue who had been sent by a magazine to interview Goonsberg, and myself, piled ourselves into Pietro Orloff's VW and headed for New Jersey to take part in this reading. On the way, somewhere beneath the Lincoln Tunnel, an argument began. About philosophy. Goonsberg kept insisting that the VW did not really exist, unless the beholder willed it to exist. This, after the teachings of Marshall McLuhan. I felt a violent rage boiling within me. He starts in again. Where is this going to lead me? I shouted that the VW sure as hell existed, and that his statements were off-the-wall. I didn't want to flip completely over this question, since I would have proved them right once again. They laughed at me, and it took everything I had to restrain myself. Then another argument began, the situation in Greece, and Papandraeou's hand in it. "Read the Sumerians," Furso insisted. I didn't see what that had to do with the discussion, and I got all worked up. Orloff drove, serenely.

We finally arrived at our destination, a little university town in New Jersey where an old friend of mine was teaching. He had organized this reading. When we entered the university coffee shop, he came to meet us, and somehow or other I ended up buying hot dogs for everyone. A political discussion began with various members of the teaching faculty, and at one point I mentioned that Furso was a Republican. "A Willkian Republican, at least?" the head of the department asked.

The reading began. After all the requisite introductions, I read a few extracts. Then Goonsberg gets started with his friend and lover, Orloff, and they sing Hindu chants. There were a series of questions, during which Furso sweated.

The evening finally came to an end, and I was able to breathe a little easier.

VII
EPISTLES

[Draft of unsent letter co-written by Carl Solomon and Allen Ginsberg in New York Psychiatric Institute.]

October 13, 1949

My dear Chevalier de Chazal:

Graciously aware of the poverty of the correspondence, and above all of its tendentious nature, between the mainland and your forlorn Indian domicile, a mere man among monsoons as you undoubtedly hold yourself to be, we have taken advantage of the favorable winds, perhaps over-abruptly, but as a last recourse, to ask for money.

We are determined upon this course only upon considering the favorable rate of exchange. If however, you have nothing but goldfish out there we will accept these, as there is a shortage of exotic goldfish in this hospital. Perhaps we are too exacting. Therefore perhaps we could justify our very inconsiderate demands on your person by inquiring if you are bald.

Uncle Malcolm, we have come upon a stupendous discovery which promises to be the work of a theology student. It would be thoughtful of you to send us a short note of encouragement a mere morsel as we are dying of hunger. We have dyed our hair purple to attract the attention of other theology students but we have met with no encouragement in the eyes of those false hearted ambassadors from Moscow, who will not stop their endless accusations of Chinoiserie.

Since our natal light comes not from China but from Mauritius we feel that you are our last resort.

Can you tell us how much you charge for a season? We can live in goldfish bowls and thereby bring in much revenue from admiring Japanese tourists.

We have poignant types of children to the number of seven.

No more need be said. Beyond a certain point there can be no spoken communication and all speech is useless.

Shirley Temple and Dagwood Bumpstead
(who affixes his name under protest)

[Draft of unsent letter co-written by Carl Solomon and Allen Ginsberg in New York Psychiatric Institute.]

December 19, 1949

[To T.S. Eliot]
Most distinguished Number 1 poet of 1949:

The year is fast running out. We wish to affirm, if we may use so banal a word, that the year is running out. Does this not frighten you?

"Uneasy wears the crown that wears the head." etc.

Now we know all about cold spots on the moon and other items that probably preoccupy you at this, shall we say turbulent?, moment, so close to Christmas as it is. We understand very well that your conversion was fraudulent. You carried it off very well. Now to get on to business.

We have here crowded into this very room, 45 potential applicants, young legislators to be from various walks of society, together packed tight, and we constitute as you must be aware, a very formidable bloc. What we want to say, though its very difficult to explain pointedly, [is] that we want to represent ourselves as your Maginot line, though it is getting late in the year. We'll make riots for you. We'll make bonfires. There you have it, 45 young legislators (incidentally, to illustrate the proselytysing vigor of our legislators, one of those has just come in and announced to us that he has just converted one John Puccio, tinker, to our cause) scurrying through the night starting—there you have it—bonfires, all over, in order to advance your candidacy under the theory (we know you will sympathize) that every vote counts.

To illustrate the quality of self-criticism in our ranks, one of our younger members has just criticised your body. You have a big nose. But we tend to regard this this way—for you to have a big nose is for us to have a big nose. (The ace of spades, the tarot cards, the dying king, the rituals and everything, we all know that.) So now to get on to business as we are legislators.

To illustrate some more of the self-criticism, another young legislator of our ranks (the same one as before, it so happens—but he is very vociferous, and is promised to a grey dramatic critic, on Broadway, America) has interjected

" 'Uneasy wears the crown that wears the head' etc. kills the whole program."

The fact is, that some 85% of our young legislators are schemers, and you cannot count on them to be real firebrands (you know our position on that, personally, and you need not worry about us, I am sure you will be gratified by us). We know exactly where you stand on the question of the existence of your great mind. We are prepared to publicly back up our charges, defying libel, lawsuits, the stupid comments of newspaper would be litterateur editorialists manque.

Certain literary dirigibles (we use the term figuratively) claim that you are a dictator. But these people have nothing to do with the main body of traditional literature, but these people are stinkers. Has a stinker ever occupied a famous place in literature, English or French? I am not speaking of Russians, as they have always been bolsheviks, even before you became a dictator.

We send our regards and highest genuflections to Mrs. Literary Dictator and all the little literary dictators. This was decided on at the last meeting, after much debate. Schwamp, who is earnest, but a fool at heart, says that you want to keep them in the background, but we know that your family is really mongoloid. But as an illustration of our total participation in your decades we voted to mention them too. This shows how completely we are of your camp.

We are waiting for marching orders. Some of our younger and less responsible young legislators to be want us to embark en masse, to China, thinking to join you there, on the theory that you'll soon contract a non-aggression pact with the reds in order to play for time. They feel our arrival there would give you an extra card up your sleeve to bargain with. The time will come when you won't have anybody to depend on but us, and young as we are, we still are legislators who know our minds and have taken a blood oath to respect you, no matter what happens. Anybody that reneges on the agreement, we will kill them. We do this with your tacit approval, in order that you need not be implicated if we get caught by the American police who are very brutal. But we vow not to involve you, because we know all about abysses already. In war there is no umpire, but nevertheless do not attempt to use your powers of divination: as regards the powers of divination, *il s'agit de guerre moderne* (Clausewitz, Rommel, etc.), but you know all that.

Now to get back to speaking of you, personally, if we may make so bold. There are no atheists in foxholes. This definitely settles the religious question. Some of our younger legislators are Jews (you don't know their names), but we have decided to treat them as if they were dopey daffodils, a special category of legislator which we have invented for your approval. They think they are all budding young Clemenceaus. Perhaps there is a place for them in France.

The meeting is fast becoming a farce, indistinguishable from a pepper steak party, the like of which was given last week, or two weeks ago at the very most, by the young Chevalier of Malcolm De Chazal, where they did nothing but eat. Therefore, much as we would like to go on chatting with you, exchanging literary gossip, news that would be of mutual interest, we will simply conclude by rephrasing a question that was made from the floor, by one of your young devotees who will not get up, whether you have epilepsy like Dostoyevski. If so (and Dostoyevski we consider from the very first to have been a dead issue, as far as this meeting is concerned—next month being set aside for our Dostoyevski memorial—) we want to know if you have not neglected it. We care for you and would be reassured that you have taken all available steps to curtail this dreadful disease which would turn you into a feebleminded mongolian idiot, too, which would make our position rather embarrassing.

Before saying farewell, we want to assure you that we know a good literary dictator when we see one: A smart young fellow like you, a real hustler.

In case you are wondering who is responsible for this transcription of the meeting, I may be permitted to speak of myself as a young poet who though passing through a position of temporary and purely transitional sterility, as far as productivity presently counts, will soon be bigger than you.

We take our leave by asking us to kiss you goodbye.

Signed,
Your 44 favorite legislators,
(one dissenting vote)
who are your brightest acolytes,
Yisraeli Soccer Team.

September 7, 1957

Dear Carl,

From a letter to your mother I recently learned of your destination in a psychiatric institution. Wrote in reply to her letter telling her that I myself spent a couple of months in such an institution. It's not such a bad place but one much better to look back upon than to think well of when you are in it. I particularly remember a cadaverous psychiatrist who had direct charge of me, a swell guy whose name I have unfortunately forgotten. I imagine that you have some such man (I hope it's a man) responsible for you. Do some exercise, even long walks through the country? That's the most beneficial thing of all. But a sympathetic psychiatrist will make up for all that.

It is not a hopeless situation for a poet as you are when things go against you. You have your family as first defense against the world. You have a brain, a damned good one from all reports; give it a chance to function. Start slow. When you feel impelled to slip, hang on to yourself by sheer dogged determination that you will not give into a slovenly thought. Sooner or later you'll find yourself able to take the next constructive step which is the secret desire of your heart, you know that, and you have made a start in your own reconstruction. Be content with that small gain and you're saved. I know it from having been through it.

You must be willing to go slow, slow, slow in a psychiatric recovery, incredibly slow, painfully slow, a minute step at a time. Every advantage that you can gain in your recovery must be seized. The thing I am here to tell is that the recovery is sure once you have started the uphill road. Good poets are necessary in our life, and you have already shown yourself to be a good one.

Best of luck to you. I hope your health keeps pace with your desires.

Sincerely yours,
(signed) William Carlos Williams

Dear Allen:

Your phone was disconnected so I had no way of knowing your whereabouts until I called your brother today. It seems I have a book for you for Christmas— Raymond Roussel's *Impressions of Africa* which is reputed to be a big surrealist classic. I bought it for myself at Ted's last month and found its mystical, cabbalistic quality to be a big drag to me at the present time, with my present concerns which require intelligent and realistic awareness of the world around me. So, I decided that you would probably get more out of the book than I did. It is a Christmas present and I hope you like it.

Mazeltov,
Carl Solomon

P.S. Let me know when you get your phone connected.

Dear Allen:

Yomolka and all I have escaped from the lunatic rathole which your perverted old auntie antics drove me into. You and your mother entered my life at a certain point. Carrying with you your entourage of Huncke, Burroughs, Kerouac, Carr and Cassady I even know Bill Gains by this time—Corso has become my brother under the lousy skin—Who was Paul Bowles to me before I met you? And Anatole and Delmore and Jaime and Henry? This craft of poetry (as it is officially known) is parasitic and we live off another's hat.

I will try to obtain your address from Leroi Jones to mail this missive. I may be in the Sahara by the next time you are home. Good luck. All is forgotten. Why the Sahara? Because I am a Saharist. Why? No dandruff. Nothing but the excelsior of the foreign breeze. The paraplegic rejoices at my Disneyesque face and so the carnival has begun again. Mummified we face the Republicans again, their pubic hairs all a-blossom.

On our foreheads are the scars of incisions. WHY the tomb? Why the tomb? WHY am I ready for the tomb? My friend Norman has just interrupted with a telephone call so I'll close.

Mon Cher Ginsberg,

"Sans les pederastes quel paradis serait ce monde, ce terre!"

That is our thought for today. I am perpetually haunted by this horror which torments my older as my younger days. Imagine if you will a world in which there was no Communism, no fumes of marijuana, no hint of sexual deviation. Where every male had a beautiful female; everybody was in the good graces of both law and custom. Instead of this gaudy horror, mixture of blood and dung which has confronted my eyes for nearly forty years. Nature moves in such strange ways, to make everything somehow imperfect and permeated with the seeds of its own decay. As for Pound contradicting himself that makes literary news and if I were still beatnik reporter for *Pilgrim's Progress*, it would make a good item. You are literary news, nothing more. You breathe publicity, no air. Any contact I ever have with you puts me in the public domain, a controversial figure. Well, such is the peculiar position into which we were placed by our juxtaposition at PI. Tout va bien. See you when you get back.

avec mes compliments à votre pere,
Carl

P.S. I do not want the presidency—what I would prefer would be to be absolute monarch with a palace made of butter-crunch candy in Kansas. I urge you to express the same preference.

[To Claude Pélieu, French author who wrote the preface to *mishaps, perhaps*.]

March 3, 1973

Mon cher Pélieu,

Je ne suis pas pederaste.
Ni frotteur.
Merci.
As regards the scene, Allen broke his leg but is now giving readings again, hobbling around in a cast. Ted Wilentz gave a party (which I attended) last week at his shop. It was a benefit for Erje Auden, the author of a Milleresque novel *The Crazy Green of Second Avenue*. Seymour Krim was co-sponsor of the party. Very pleasant. Friends of Ted, bookstore people, assorted bohemians

young and old. Peter, Allen, Arlene Dahlberg, Ann Waldman and her mother.

Me? I do heavy work at Korvette's department store. Diet books outselling sex books, but both selling well. Fiction not so much. *Jonathan Livingston Seagull* top fiction. Huncke apparently living quietly in NY. Irving Rosenthal still around. Saw movie in NY called *It Happened in Hollywood*. Produced by *Screw* newspaper. Sodomy and blow jobs. Muggings and crime on street all over. Civilization a joke. No integrity, no truth anywhere. World's problems insoluble. Artaud's screams reverberate. Last voice of honesty in civilization becoming more stupid every year. Eat, fuck; eat, suck. Work, work, work. My beard finally white at bottom. Not an Extinguished Poet yet.

Julius back in bughouse. Has little job there. Read your book *Infra Noir*. I am not really Carl-le-Momo. Momo just another bullshit pose to avoid solitude by imagining that one has Momo brothers or Momo group to belong to. Rigaut said nothing that cardiac condition doesn't say more effectively. Ann well. Regards to Mary. Love from this old-timer.

Carl Solomon

[To Jacqueline Starer, French scholar.]

February 26, 1975

Dear Jacqueline,

Unfortunately, I have no unpublished material on hand at present. I am writing very little at present and am embedded in a very unadventurous routine that involves holding a bookselling job and seeing certain special friends at certain intervals. My ideas consist largely in what emerges from the dialogues with these few friends—and relatives, neighbors and co-workers. The odds are always against one. One's well-being always looms as a threat to others. Only when one is ill, do they become sympathetic. The ideal state would be neither to be too well or too sick. This involves no threat to others. So I have been getting well and getting sick since 1948; going into asylums and being cured of insanity and royally welcomed to the city since that time. A thoroughly boring business and an utter waste of time. My feeling is that the advent of nuclear energy and the raising of the spectre of Armageddon ushered in our age of anxiety and our Beat Generation—or generations. A static world situation leaves no alternative but continuous nervousness. Right? Mr. Ginsberg and Mr. Kerouac and perhaps even Mr. Antonin Artaud shared our malady and were our co-sufferers. Also Mr. Bob Hope. I see nobody as a winner or loser and this afternoon, as I write, I feel quite satisfied with Mr. T. S. Eliot's description of life as a matter merely of "Birth, copulation, and death." In my present life, I am very much "with it." What other alternative?

By the way, I just read Laquuer's *Weimar*—a cultural history of pre-Hitler Germany.

My best to you,
Carl Solomon

May 21, 1975

Dear Allen,

A word or two on mental and physical meanderings since I saw you last. First of all, let me ask, "How is your health?" After all, it was only about ten years ago that we decided we wanted to see the year 2000. Come what may. Derangement or disease or disaster notwithstanding.

As for me, I went back on the regular dose of tranquilizers and have felt good ever since. Went to see the "Sheila Levine" movie with Elaine and decided it was lousy. Ate raspberry ices in Rumpelmyer's.

Read a short novelette about a mentally ill New York kid and realized how hard it is to write well about mental illness.

The John Cage thing, by the way, was amazing. He just sat there muttering or cooing, I don't know which, and the audience giggled, snored, sat in what was probably puzzlement. I found myself wondering whether or not John Cage uses foot powder. Not that his feet smelled. I certainly couldn't smell him from where I was sitting, but you know how the mind wanders when the performer doesn't hold your attention.

I have been having stirring, fascinating dreams. I have been dreaming of a wild, sin-town named Coptic—like Brecht's Mahagonny—how I and a group of patients from Pilgrim escaped from Pilgrim and hid out in Coptic, in fact went beyond it—then were forced by circumstance to backtrack. A schism broke out among us; some wanted to go back to the hospital (me included) and others wanted to continue the escape trek into New York. Then I woke up. This afternoon, I dreamed a dream in which you and Tuli Kupfenberg figured. Expressionist drama involving such dream-characters as The Afghanistan Kid and The Dole Kid. I don't interpret these dreams. I just enjoy them.

I also dreamed what I must consider as an anti-Communist dream. My friend Eugene, acting very authoritarian and commissar-like, came upon me suddenly and asked, "Why haven't you been helping Juan with his cobbling work?" I hadn't been helping Juan and couldn't help feeling that Eugene's regime was repressive and not the sort of thing I liked. Sort of not the set-up in which I could flourish or enjoy myself.

Carl Solomon

June 30, 1975

Dear Allen,

"Hieronymo has gone mad againe." This quotation from "The Wasteland" should be a fair indication to you that in spite of the many personal transactions I have been involved in since our original hieratic communication, I have not entirely forgotten the Olympian world of English poetry—or American. My job is in danger. My sanity is danger. I am smoking too much. I am dreaming bizarre dreams. Will I be bounced from my safe niche into a world of flagellantes and coxcombs again? Have I sized up things wrong and committed the cardinal sin of making a series of horrendous misjudgments again? As you see my *spelling* is still good. What more does the world want of me? As a boy, I won spelling bees. Why does 1975 not treat me with the respect that 1937 did? May I, with your permission, flee to Cherry Valley, if the going gets too rough? Remember the summer of the McGovern campaign. You shielded me from the news that I had been fired during my vacation. I came back and within three helter-skelter weeks I found another job. Held it since then steadfastly. Another crisis seems building up on this one and with a little generosity among us all, your friend (me) may come through this one with less anxiety than the last. Perhaps, in my mind I am exaggerating the danger to my worldly fortunes. But one never knows, does one? I hope this note finds you well. I had a brief communication with Bill regarding the broadcast we made. Write to me. Mother sends regards.

Tenderness and such rot,
Carl Solomon

August 5, 1975

Hello Allen,

How are you feeling? I wrote to Gordon that I don't like the two pieces and I told him I don't want them reprinted. You can throw a tantrum if you like. I don't see what good your hysterical imagery is doing anybody. Danny Greenfield (who was at PI when we were, though you probably don't remember him) ran into me in Korvette's where he was shopping. The poor guy (I despised him at that time) has had a lobotomy since then in addition to the topectomy (operation through the eye) which he'd been given at PI. We were friendly and mutually sympathetic this time and he remembers you as my friend there. He asked about you without my mentioning you. I told him you'd become a world-famous poet during the 25 years since we'd last met. He said, "Gee!"

No more finagling by you or your meatball anti-Semitic friend Corso.

I love you as ever (and wish it were mutual—proven by deed rather than by mournful and forlorn eulogy) and am going up to your farm to swim and fish in Solomon Pond August 18–25.

As for courses on French poets of the World War II

era, frankly I would rather forget about them and think of the pleasant things of life—*which are abundant*. With me, life comes about 3000 miles before art.

> Your old pal met somewhere along life's way,
> Carl Solomon

P.S. Elaine and my mother send regards—really.

November 9, 1976

Dear Allen,

The Carter victory made us very happy. My mother, I, Elaine, and Denise all voted for Carter. In the past couple of days, I became aware of three deaths all of which had some meaning for me. First, Anna Kavan, a writer of the Djuna Barnes type whose "Asylum Piece" I read while receiving treatment at PI. She died of a self-administered OD. Then, Joseph Starobin, who had been an editor of the *Daily Worker* and whom I had heard lecture at CCNY when I was a student there in the mid-forties. He was 62. And further, Baron Gottfried von Cramm, the German tennis star of the thirties who had been exposed as a homosexual in Hitler's Germany. This had been the first exposé of a celebrity as a homosexual in my lifetime and, at that time, it had seemed remote and mysterious indeed. Our entire era, the era covered by our life-spans, is vanishing piece by piece, increasingly larger chunks of it vanishing as each year passes—until we ourselves will have vanished. There is a new $20 Artaud biography-study, introduced by Susan Sontag—the most pretentious to date. Large review in the Sunday

Times. They say he wasn't really all that bright but that his life was monumental in the excruciating suffering he absorbed. He died at 52. I feel the *Times*' appraisal of Artaud's career was a good objective one—time has necessarily corrected earlier distortions. Do you know anything about the German poet Hölderlin? He, according to my encyclopedia, went mad at 33, spent the rest of his life in asylums and died at 73. Amazing? Glad you liked my poem. I am no longer overweight. Strict diet. Looking forward to your return. Best to Pietro.

Carl Solomon

October 18, 1986

Dear Allen,

This one-page piece (I had hoped it would be longer, but I am unaccountably nervous this afternoon and was eager to get the job done quickly) is not based on any research other than that which has come my way in the course of leading my "soi-disant" normal life in New York City in recent months. Such quality of life makes explicable to me the reluctance of State Hospital patients during years past to rejoin the communities they had left before entering the hospitals. It really took courage to "go home," considering what those homes were. Again I apologize for the brevity, but feel that it is a sufficiently typical sampling of experience to give you an idea of what one goes through as a slightly below average New York City wage-earner at this juncture in our history.

Carl Solomon

[This letter and the one following are from novelist John Clellon Holmes.]

June 15, 1987

Dear Carl:

Allen seems to have broadcast my baddish news to the winds, which is okay because it occasioned a letter from you. First one I've ever received. "The nervous puff," indeed! One too many of those, it seems.

I've been hard at work, despite the fact (or perhaps because of the fact) that I can't talk intelligibly anymore. I make a series of sounds that resemble an obscure Urdu dialect as spoken by the "natives" of Monogram Films in the 1940s. I scribble notes. And I type.

Did you know that the University of Arkansas Press will publish a three-volume edition of my non-fiction in the next years? An unlikely circumstance, but true. The first, *Displaced Person: The Travel Essays*, will be out in November. The second, *Representative Men: The Biographical Essays*, should be out in early 1988. The third, which I've just begun assembling, will probably be called *Passionate Opinions: Essays in the Culture*, and should appear sometime in 1989. All told well over 1000 pages of manuscript prepared for publication in a trifle over a year. Much new stuff, much rewriting, some rethinking. We'll see what happens. Also, there's a slim book of recent poetry, *Dire Coasts*, due this November from a small press in Idaho. Anyway, you can see my hands haven't been idle.

After the years of teaching and wandering, it's good to be home again, in the house we've lived in off and on for 30 years, here in New England where they have seasons and deep water and fish. Didn't realize how homesick I'd become after a decade in deepest Dixie. Ironic, of course, that all these difficulties should have struck me at this juncture, but I've no long thoughts about it. Luck or lack of it, I suppose. I find that so far I've had no revelations, one way or the other. Do I lack the imagination to be a believer? Anyway, I'm in no real sweat about any of it yet.

I managed to avoid all passionate baseball attachments for most of my life, and don't believe I'll form any now. I expended my sports-energy on the America's Cup. Anyway, keep all flags flying, Carl. Isn't Time the oddest kink of all?

Ever,
John

October 5, 1987

Dear Carl:

Just out of hospital for tracheotomy (the Liz Taylor wound to the throat), and vow never to go into slammer again.

Yes, I was in a hospital once, down in Dixie, when the platelets in my blood had vanished due to bad diet or something, and my potassium level was nil, and I had all the symptoms of having had a cerebral accident, was out of my usually ordered head, and I was routinely asked every morning what my name was, where I was, and what was the date. I didn't cheat and so flunked the test for three days. No way to cheat; no newspaper, and I was convinced the TV had been "bugged" to drive me crazy. Well-a-day . . .

I'm just getting back to editing a volume of journal-entries for Paragon, having just this minute finished the last volume of the *Selected Essays* project. The first comes out in two weeks.

They're holding another mammoth Kerouac-bash in

Quebec right now, to which I was asked a long while ago, but had to turn it down because I can't speak at all now, I'm quite dumb, and even the few sounds I make no longer sound (as they did for a while) like the obscure Central Casting tongue that natives in the Poverty Row Tarzan movies of the mid-thirties used to speak. Now I'm mytherously wordless. (I'll let that spelling stand).

Anyway, I was looking forward to prowling around Quebec City, never been there. But instead I'll stay home to see a VCR copy of Hitchcock's *I Confess*. Confess to having a lowering energy level these days, so being flat on my back for a while has its appeal. Anyway, just thought I'd say hello. I'm weeks behind in answering letters, and found your last one in the stack, and thought a good thought of you.

take care,
John

[Kay Vorhies met Carl Solomon at the twenty-fifth anniversary celebration of the publication of *On The Road* in Boulder, Colorado in 1982.]

September 13, 1985

Dear Kay,

This is Friday the thirteenth. Furthermore, I am an Aries. I don't know what you are. Astrology went out with Jimmy Carter. Happy birthday anyway. I didn't relish the idea of turning thirty when that occurred in my life either. It meant goodbye to so much youth stuff. However, what you must be beginning to realize is that you go right on juggling this youth and age stuff around so long as you remain coherent. I must have been pretty young when I read Eliot's "Gerontion" the first time. And some kids have the eyes of wise old men. What happens in "second childhood" I have yet to discover. At what age is it stylish to be cynical? I really don't dig cynicism much at present. Go more for nostalgia and twilight-sentimental moods.

One of the Kerouac movies we made in Boulder three years ago is playing at the Bleecker Cinema. I appear in it briefly. It's quite a good account of Kerouac's life, I think.

Our friendship of three years has been a good one. You found work, didn't starve; I found work and gave up smoking. Got heavier and some color in my cheeks. There is another messenger who is rather a well known poet. Steve Tropp. He works for my company. Thursday, I was walking down Wall Street with my messages and who do I behold standing and reading a paperback novel right on the sidewalk but Steve Tropp? I said to him, "Steve, you're a messenger, you're not a publisher's reader."

Where to from here? Well, maybe to an all NY World Series. I really have the world at my fingertips and if I complain about it not being overly interesting it is probably not the poor old world's fault.

I read *The Nation* every week in order to be slightly subversive. Which is what I desire to be. Only slightly. Only a shade. This makes me feel I'm still fun to be with.

Love,
Carlos Amigo

October 4, 1985

Dear Kay,

Bits of philosophy perhaps useful to us here in neurotic 1985. My late father, big hero of World War I (ma-

chine-gunner, wounded in leg, who used to describe bay-
onet warfare to me at age 6 or 7), was given to saying:
you only die once. William Burroughs at Naropa said:
The ship is sinking, it's every man for himself. Jean-Paul
Sartre, old dead existentialist playwright wrote in a
play before you were born (one character's line): "Hell
is other people." Sartre's character's phrase is truest,
though. People are never done hassling us. Did Dean
see it that way? I never knew much about Dean (didn't
even see *Rebel Without a Cause*) because I was busy trying
to dig the life of lunatics in the mental hospital while
he (Dean) was having a vogue of a kind in the outside
world. My philosophy throughout my boring life, including nuthouse, has been "When's chow?" Even at Naropa,
and even now messengering for a few years, as you've
probably been able to deduce from all the references to
taste thrills in my letters, I have probably lived to eat
rather than the reverse. And, believe me, a good bowel
movement leaves the head clear for philosophy like
nothing else.

Went fishing with Allen and Ted Morgan, *ecrivain
français*, last week. No fish. They'd been driven out to sea
by Hurricane Gloria.

Remember me while you roam. Regards to Steve,
whom I've seemed to have diligently refrained from
mentioning.

Love,
Carl

P.S. Julian Beck, big man in avant-garde theater died
recently. Did you read? Our old NY scene is losing its
old-timers very rapidly. I did a review of Jules Laforgue's
Tales and it got lost at the St. Mark's Church. I had no
duplicate. It wasn't half bad either. Will have a poem in
fall or winter *Oink*—poem from 20 years ago.

January 25, 1986

Dear Kay,

Continuing to run my old age home with intelligence and compassion for as long as will prove necessary. Yes, the world picture does at times seem threatening. The Third World with nukes, the AIDS epidemic, and other evils seem to pile up—but as I indicated in my last letter, nothing can get me thoroughly downhearted if I can get to a nice piece of cake with chocolate icing every so often. I have always loved to eat. I just ate one and am at the moment licking my lips. Religion helps at times, though I wouldn't be too specific about which religion—and equally helpful at times are throwing off the religious do's and don'ts.

Doing the crossword puzzle is something I too often substitute on Sunday for going to religious services which I also do on some Sundays, Jewish in my case. And to add further to the apparent muddlement is the fact that I am going to a current events forum in March at a Marxist school, the forum conducted by a very acerbic left-wing writer named Alexander Cockburn whose work appears in *The Nation* magazine. Can't define myself but move through the world with a shuffling gait dodging brickbats and having what, to me, is fun.

Lettrism? You remember the post-World War I avant-garde, which was revolutionary and threw off all the shackles of convention? Well, after the Second World War all that groundwork had already been done and there were in fact very few shackles still to be broken, very few taboos still untouched—so what emerged were a number of limited cults dedicated to somewhat new wrinkles and generally extending the work already done in the twenties. Here there was a lot of Reichian therapy; there was the bebop cult in music; in Europe, existential philosophy, post-surrealism like Artaud, Michaux, etc. and in poetry a new cult which was called lettrism. Rimbaud liberated the word; Isadore Isou the founder of lettrism liberated the letter. He has a group, and after forty years they still meet. Apparently, at this stage of this movement, it is a sort of aesthetic anarchism whose members cling tightly together and militantly nonconform to their French brothers and sisters. One of their publicists whom I know compares them to the punks. They are old stuff to me. I discovered them in '47.

So it goes. Big dental job just finished. Still messengering.

Love,
Carl

April 12, 1986 Saturday morning

Dear Kay,

I received your pro-gangster letter and can only reply with a platitude: Everything is relative. I have had my phases of being interested in gangsters, the most recent being in post-World War II Paris when I was the steady customer of a French prostitute named Odette. We used to have our rendez-vous in a Montmarte bar called "The Grand Duc" and an occasional customer was a man called Armand le Fou. On one occasion he took out a revolver and began firing at somebody. I never knew what happened amid all the confusion, but Odette later described Armand to me as a *"mauvais garcon"* (rotten egg) and hinted to me that he was some kind of gangster. Those were the days when I was drawn into the ambience of Jean Genet, of whom I am sure you have heard.

As a child I was given to playing cops-and-robbers (a game we had) in which I would alternate roles and sometimes be a law-and-order hero and sometimes a desperado. We also had cowboy and Indian games in which we again alternated roles—before this giving rise to my adult political ambivalence. I can't recall Roman and Christian games or British and Hindu games, but they probably would have been a lot of fun too. I shall try to checkout the B. Traven tale and of course would be titillated by anything about your love life, recent or past, that you care to reveal. During the AIDS epidemic I have more or less given up sensual pursuits in favor of a renewed interest in comparative religions.

Love,
Carl

May 31, 1986

Dear Kay,

Your letters, since 1982, have become an essential part of my life since that time. I remember my enthusiasm for John Irving's writing at that time, when I was generally somewhat morose. Now it seems that John Irving has not had much to say since *Garp* and I am considerably less morose.

As the years have passed, season by season, we have moved along and have both, at least, shared in the collective experience of these times: the pennant races, the elections, the plants flowering, the summit conferences, the unwinding of my parent's senescence.

Another summer coming up. Your latest jaunt should give rise to some interesting letters. Allen is in Mississippi where one of his friends, Gordon Ball, is teaching at the university. I go on fishing a little, visiting my mother at the nursing home, messengering, taking care of my uncle (86 years old). I just read a book on retirement planning, dealing with the management of IRA accounts and so forth. Old age and death are subjects I will probably be having more and more contact with as the years go by. I have no children, but at least I have the rampaging Mets to make my later years happy. There are always substitutes for real things. I've been reading the New Testament and attending Jewish services and have found that it is perfectly all right to have nothing to say in the course of conducting these religious activities. They make me the enemy of no one, not atheists, not Muslims. Camus' "indifferent universe" shines through, though I do have an occasional political reaction to whatever is going on. So on.

Love,
Carl

[To George Montgomery, rustic poet and Kerouac enthusiast.]

Dear George,

If nothing else, I've gained considerable Life Experience. Who else could have begun *War and Peace* at 12 and finished it at 40? Who else could have caught dozens of sand porgies out on the Island at 6? Who else could have dumped garbage overboard during storms at sea on the North Atlantic at 18? Who else could have met Allen Ginsberg? Who else could have worked in the nuthouse bakery and then proceeded to date Barbara Moraff? Who else could have read at the Metro and then risen to become assistant manager of the Korvette's Fifth Avenue book department? Who else could have given up smoking and then become a veteran messenger for the same company Steve Tropp works for, carrying packages for Rupert Murdoch and transporting a pair of spectacles from George Plimpton to a friend of his? Who else is the North Bronx's answer to Paul Bunyan?

Still going strong and unless fate intervenes, for many years to come. I took a leave of absence this week to help my mother and am sitting and reading (1) Norman Mailer's latest novel and (2) a book I bought in the Argosy bookstore by Irving Babbitt, written in 1912—well-written criticism about the likes of Hippolyte Taine and St. Beuve. It's a delight to read old books because of their stylistic felicities.

What new worlds have we to conquer? Will there be a human race after the AIDS epidemic?

You are interested in trivia. Well, there was a trivia man on the corner of Wall and Broadway one Friday evening last summer after work and I answered one of his questions. (What was the first baseball team? Answer: the Cincinnati Red Stockings.)

You asked for a letter. This is it.

Carl Solomon
October 31, 1985

[The following two letters were written to John Tytell.]

Independence Day, 1986

Dear John,

I am doing as I promised. Hereby, a letter. Saw the first six innings of the July Fourth Mets game at Shea, left the park in the sixth inning, went to see Mom at the nursing home. On way, I met a sweet PR chick who is into poetry, knew of Notzake Shange, etc. and she will accept my offer to take her fishing. About 22 years old and I felt strong attraction physically. I received the Ginsberg festschrift. There is no piece by you in it, but, never despair, I do recall coming across your name in a piece on Cherry Valley by Gordon Ball (unless I am mistaken —I often make mistakes). The author refers to you as a cultural historian. Real crafty label. You are my friend the cultural historian.

Dig these tactics: I used my in with Harper and Row via the *Annotated Howl* route to be sent the outfit's proofreading test by the copyeditor. Should arrive soon. If I acquit myself well I am to send a background bit with emphasis on Ace Books mss. reading stint (20 years?) to have my name put on file for proofreading assignment. I am so nervous about all this that my heart is beating like Poe's tell-tale organ.

How's Danby?

> Be carefree
> (instead of the conventional "take
> care"),
>
> > > Carl S.

July 18, 1986

Dear John,

To your handwritten note, I reply with another. I'm vacationing in the Bronx: fishing, job-searching, nursing home visiting, baseball watching, gossiping, agonizing. Finally getting a chance to read good literature. Reading Tennessee Williams' short stories. By the way, the festschrift mention of you was in Al Aronowitz's piece, not Gordon Ball's—as I had stated.

American Book Review breaks records for non-payment. Even Arthur Knight sent me $25 for the interview.

The world of beatnikry recedes from public view as cocaine hogs all the headlines. Leave it to mankind to find the easy way out of troubles.

Enjoy your leisure,
Carl Solomon

VIII
FUGITIVE POEMS

POETRY

Most poetry today is either boring, incomprehensible or both. I prefer poetry which is attempting to make some sort of philosophic point. It must be backed up by a theory, or illustrate a theory to really interest me. If it lacks a hard core of ideas, then it is merely words. The reason I feel why poetry is made to submit to psychiatry today (and philosophy as well) is that this science offers theories and ideas while poetry (since surrealism) does not. Poets turn more and more to theories (way *in* or way *out*) of mental health since psychiatry now seems the queen of intellectual disciplines. Ours has really become a world without poetry and that is why our cities now look like open-air asylums. The cops (attendants) herd the kooks around the city blocks like vast wards. There is absolutely no difference anymore between living outside a hospital and in one. I do not know what to write to restore your equilibrium other than to suggest that you engage in physical labor (if you haven't already).

SECRET THOUGHTS ABOUT ALLEN

He goes on writing.
Reams and reams of paper with
    more talk on it.
What can he find to say?
My mind dwells on long-gone

themes like the scuttling of the Graf Spee.
And how dead things are
And about how when I stare out at
the stars, they still stare back.
And the transcience of life; how
Kerouac is gone and my publishing uncle
is gone and David Burnett is gone
and Marianne Moore is gone.
And my mind dwells on the wisdom of the
patient at the Institute who
when asked "What's new?" asked
in reply, "What should be new?"

HEROIC POET

The one who,
Tied up in a strait jacket,
Suavely excuses himself,
"Don't bother me now, I'm all tied up."

FOREIGN AID SUGGESTION

Why not
large shipments
of alphabet
soup to

areas of widespread
illiteracy?

RAISON D'ETRE FOR OTHERWISE EMPTY POETS

1

sit and speculate
on the nature of the
twenty-first century
already in sight.
Well, the world will not have
been destroyed by atomic holocaust as
some feared in mid-twentieth,
I hope.
Merely,
ploys
and
détentes
and
confrontations
At the moment
the word seems to be
COLD WAR FOREVER
with limited actions
no Armageddon.
Another 34 years of nervousness
And then the twenty-first
Empty poets, there you have your
raison d'être—to survive until the twenty-first!
At the end of the nineteenth there were

a plethora of prophets.
Now there are few. Who knows what to expect?
I sit and wait, my hand on the TV button.

BEHIND THE TIMES

Nobody Tells Me the Truth Anymore

In this dour day
Of tranquilizing pills
Diarrhea
The white negro
The criticism of criticism
The ideological split between Peking and Moscow
And Parataxic Distortions
I am at a loss to find
Any personal truth
And am left with
A philosophic relativism
Which renders me utterly incapable of
Expressing myself
With any degree of honesty
This honesty which had been
My primary characteristic as a boy
And which had me far afield in my search
For truth.
Of such stuff is intellectual tragedy made.

NARY A LOUSE

Oh, you don't find the louse in literature anymore
But I remember the days when you did
They added a certain roguish piquancy
To the work of Queneau
("The Skin of Dreams"), Artaud
(les morpions
de l'eternite), and Henry Miller
You see we took the advice of our critics
And took that all-important bath
Now there is only the surrealism of gleaming teeth
I haven't seen a louse in twenty years
But I am left with the feeling that their hideous presence
Once influenced our literature
And played a significant role
In producing those mid-century works
Of Despair and disgust
That we were weaned upon
And that we can never duplicate
Now that our romanticism has
Vanished in
A cold shower

I'M A GUY WHO WRITES NOTHING BUT SLIM VOLUMES

Look at my last one.
Look at it.
Do you like it?
I'm leaving for Zanzibar in a few minutes.

How I've suffered!
Are you following me?
I think I'll hit the road.

THE BORING REVOLUTION

People stand around and hold cocktails
Or dance.
Yet, they are constantly talking of revolution.
How come?
Why the infatuation with this daring word?
The paperback revolution, the sexual revolution,
the fashion revolution, the Negro revolution.
It is definitely the world's favorite word, to be called
upon when others evoke no response.
It frightens, it chills, it makes one feel dangerous
no matter how meek one looks—and is.
And always the same thing: nothing happens except
that the tracts and broadsides and paperbacks pile up in
a corner.

THE ROCK 'N' ROLL GENERATION
GOES BALD

Someone came to tell me that Ed Sanders had lost his
   hair.

Now that's symptomatic.
I expect to see the entire rock'n' roll generation,
with its long hair,
wearing wigs one fine day.
Oh, the fleeting melancholy!

IX
REVIEWS

RATHER REICH THAN RESIDENT

The Burning Glass
by John Franklin Bardin

John Franklin Bardin emerges from his first serious novel as a lineal descendant of the early Douglas, the early Huxley and the early Connolly in a now almost abandoned vein of mordant intellectual satire. Few will deny that the tradition of Nepenthe and of the rock pool, shallow and smugly unobtrusive as it was, has been trodden deep into the dirt by the international conflagration and the onslaughts of the New Criticism and bebop. Nevertheless, Mr. Bardin has undertaken its salvage in a manner which claims our attention if only because of its inadequacy.

His novel, having many of the qualities of the *roman à thèse*, is built around a plot which is comparatively simple and is adorned with a minimum of structural nuance. It concerns the journey of a young married couple, she a poetess and he a geneticist, to an archetypical summer colony, and traces the crisis which suddenly arises in their relationship through to its ultimate resolution. The cause of the crisis is, at first, obscured in their minds by the bitterness of their conflict and by the seemingly great distance separating their respective private visions. She is obsessed with an ambiguous poetic image of birth and death, he with his quest for pink-eyed drosophilae. Driven apart for a day, both come to mingle with their more disturbed neighbors, who have the habit of acting out their conflicts with sometimes fatal and always sordid results. Thus, by virtue of their juxtaposition with this bloodstained backdrop, the two quarreling lovers find

themselves in similar positions—they have become ob-
servers and critics of the inept and flesh-embodied dreams
of others. At once, they become capable of distinguishing
dream from reality and they recoil in horror at the thought
of the predicament that would have awaited them had
they become entirely lost in their visions. They make love,
decide to have a child, glue the drosophila to a slide and
the poem to a printed page. Each has grasped the kernel
of universal truth in the personal dream and has sepa-
rated it from the primordial chaff.

Norman Douglas, Aldous Huxley, and Cyril Connolly killed their summertime cranks with benevolent de-
tachment, heavy with drink. Mr. Bardin kills his with
heavy and violent sympathy, with midwifely warmth; to
the naked eye, he is not a snob. With what righteous
indignation does one of his characters, Alicia Bailey, smash
to smithereens her husband's malefic Sexone Box! (For
the first time in the history of American letters the reader
actually sees the inside of one of these things.) Mr. Bardin's position is a superficially sound one. He proves by
demonstration that the poem is a lie, that one cannot live
a lie, that in order to live one must slough off the inevitable fairy tale conscientiously and live, thereafter, on
unabstracted love (too seldom is he aware that the lie, any
lie, is always a dream of love).

But the questions, couched in calypso rhythms, soon
arise, "Is his burning glass concave or convex? And if it
is neither, why is he so preoccupied with the clumsiness
of sex?" Why are his sympathetic characters and spokes-
men, in what appears to be a thesis novel, so garishly
unreal? Why is the poem they have sloughed off such a
bad one, one so unenticing, and why are we led to sympathize with and to genuinely pity those he debunks—
the Reichian, the poseur, the psychotic child-artist, whose
poems smack of transfigured life? Why does he comfort
those who need no comfort (who had no poem to live
with in the first place) and deny even a muted hope of
redemption to those who are wretched (who only under-

take to live their poems in desperation, when they see that their poems cannot be made liveable)? Is the author's midwifely warmth thus misplaced because it is factitious? I suspect, on the basis of the novel, that this is so. Mr. Bardin has attempted to rescue the rescuer, who is in this metaphor an obsolete attitude, rather than the victim, the original victim who is still the victim, drowning in seas surrounding Nepenthe, heavy with drink. In his plea for domestic felicity, he evades the burning issue, that of the survival of poetry and of myth (of the white lie, if you prefer) in an unreceptive age, by asserting the livability of the poems of poetasters rather than of those of poets, poems which he tends to regard as mistakes, as *unfortunate* lies rather than as noble and potentially rewarding ones. It is as though, in shattering the illusions of the *avant-garde*, he has come to flatter the middlebrow and has lacked the pugnacity (perhaps Promethean under present circumstances) to make the long and exhausting, but essential, effort to reconcile the two in a human synthesis —to act as interpreter.

How pollyannish and wishfully contrived seems his resolution in retrospect! And what a poor excuse it provides for the accompanying burlesque of an alienated intelligentsia—for Mr. Bardin does not ridicule the bohemian but, on the contrary, further damns him. In this sense, and at this time in this place, he is even more the social propagandist than he is the satirist.

December 4, 1950

MOTHER GOOSED . . . AND MORE

Dirty Books for Little Folks
A Chimney Sweep Comes Clean
Raging Joys, Sublime Violations
by Chandler Brossard

The first of the three books consists of a reworking of various Mother Goose nursery rhymes into pornographic parables. For example, "Jack the Giant Killer" turns into a wild tale about a male hustler named Jack peeing into the ear of a silly and lustful gay giant. "Hansel And Gretel," "Little Red Riding Hood," "The Pied Piper of Hamlin" and other nursery rhymes are similarly reworked into stories of fetishism, rapine, incest, and so forth. The effect is moderately amusing and highly scatological and sometimes one wonders whether the humor really requires such an effusion of obscenity. Brossard, though, seems to revel in it like a Rabelais or a Legman or an Ed Sanders.

I remember early Brossard from his first contribution to *Neurotica*—an essay on typical highbrow cocktail parties which was considerably more polished if more restrained than this. As a matter of fact, his early style, as in his post-war novel, *Who Walk In Darkness*, was rather Hemingwayish and verbally spare. He wrote then about Greenwich Village hipsters or existentialists (very roman à clef). The relaxation of censorship left Brossard free to engage in rambunctious psychosexual fantasy as complex and farfetched as early Genet.

In *Raging Joys, Sublime Violations*, political satire and scatological fantasy dealing for the most part with the Vietnam War are mixed together into a rather insane brew in which plot is impossible to determine or follow while characters like Allen Dulles and Mao Tse-tung and Adolf Hitler cavort on its pages raping and mauling one another. Bits of beatnik lore are thrown in, like one character killing his wife with a bow-and-arrow while doing a "William Tell" stunt, shooting an apple off her head.

Illustrative prose passage from *Raging Joys*:

> Down at the end of the bug-eyed steam table, behind which grinning lackies from the "Good Ship Lollipop" slithered in vestigial ecstacy, Bobbie Komer and Gen. Westmoreland were knee-deep in top secret badinage. The General's chin was smeared with egg (but that is merely prima facie evidence). "What you guys at the CIA need is a good spitball pitcher," said the general, licking red-eye off his fingers. "Get rid of that dinge slow baller you got now. Cause between you and me, as a result of our buildup and success, we are able to plan and initiate a general offensive. We now have gained the tactical initiative and are conducting . . ."

Neurotica, where I first encountered Brossard in the early fifties, had an all-embracing theme: a sort of Freudian examination of a culture that seemed then to be manifesting (at least in the opinions of the writers) some pathological symptoms. One may ask now: who were those writers to so judge this society and what on earth were their qualifications? Even from a mental health standpoint, the early *Neurotica* would be easily challenged today—if not altogether meaningless. The writers themselves have all gone separate ways and today nothing at all binds any of us together other than the fact that we may still have searching minds and still find this a nerveracking society to live in.

However, there is not now and perhaps never was a common philosophical or political link among those writers. Brossard, like the others I have since come across, comes up with some very odd stuff which is generally redeemed by one virtue: a don't-give-a-damn Célinish or Millerish attitude toward the Western urban cultures he wanders through as a first-person, picaresque hero. *A Chimney Sweep Comes Clean*, which takes place in England, has its examinations of the toilet habits of patrons of public urinals and similar roguery which sometimes makes for good fun but more often is generally overdone. It is the most recently written of the three books and leaves one with a kind of Orwellian feeling. The reveling in dirty words is here too but it does not come through with the singularity of effect that Henry Miller did in the days before porn was so easy to come by. One aspect of Brossard's writing that is healthy, I think, is the fact that this is not *slick* porn. There is nothing commercial or machine-made about it. The reader has the feeling that it is honest reaction to everyday phenomena by a rather literary but sensitive individual. Unpackaged porn.

In the days right after the war, existentialism was a mysterious word that had vaguely to do with something called *"moeurs"*—manners. And if Brossard was one of the earliest domestic existentialists, he has found plenty of subject matter in the bizarre manners he has encountered in various parts of the world since those early days. I know myself that the early world of Brossard, centering around the San Remo and other Greenwich Village bars, was very narrow and self-enclosed and that once you left it, you had need of very different sorts of guide books and phrase books. The Remo is gone; the characters of Brossard's roman à clef are gone—dead and gone to a certain extent—but he remains an unreconstructed anarchist—a Remo habitué in the Age of Reagan—and his greatest virtue is what some may see as his greatest flaw—a refreshing lack of professionalism. The early *Neurotica* crowd were not writers per se but mavericks just like this and this quality makes him worth reading in this day of generic books.

THE ONLY GOOD POET IS
A DEAD POET

Paul Celan: Poems
Selected, Translated and Introduced by
Michael Hamburger

The introduction to this selection of poems by Paul Celan mentions that the poet died by drowning, a suicide, ten years ago at the age of forty-nine. Here now is a beautiful volume of extremely cryptic poems by this evidently very unhappy poet brought forth with all the belated attention accompanying works by a Van Gogh, or, perhaps, a Sylvia Plath. Necrophilia is still clearly an acceptable literary pastime and the book is priced at $20.00 a copy. In the press, one reads these days of murders resulting from disputes over anything from $.50 to $10.00. The price of these hard-to-decipher poems could very well motivate two murders on today's market. Working at the minimum wage, one would have to schlep for five hours to earn enough to pay for a copy.

One must continually refer to the introduction to find anything to say about the poems which, themselves, offer very little food for thought and, by the way, are completely devoid of sexual references. So one learns that Celan had paranoid tendencies and was deeply hurt by accusations of plagiarism from the widow of Yvan Goll, the Franco-German surrealist poet. I happen to have read a volume of Goll's poems, *Jean Sans Terre*, some 18 years ago, and recall that Goll's poems were clear, beautiful and gem-like, reminding me somewhat of Yeats' Crazy Jane poems. I did not derive such pleasure from a reading of these Celan poems and do not see much ground for plagiarism charges other than that Celan may have plagiarized Goll's melancholy tone. In this sense, hundreds of

224 · EMERGENCY MESSAGES

thousands of contemporary New Yorkers currently share in this plagiarism. These poems are not nearly as well wrought as Goll's and it would be hard to find any structural similarities.

Read further in the introduction and you will learn that Celan, born into a Jewish family in Bukovina (Romania) in 1920, became a friend of Martin Heidegger, the pro-Nazi existentialist philosopher. A fact apparently hard to reconcile with another, that Celan had been a concentration camp inmate and had survived a period in David Rousset's "Other Kingdom," the Ubu-like world of the camps. One poem, emerging from the stew of Celan's history, is dedicated to Paul Eluard (dadaist-surrealist-communist) and mentions little other than the color of Eluard's eyes (blue). Michael Hamburger, author of the introduction, relates Celan's work to that of Rilke and Hölderlin. So far as Hölderlin is concerned, it is true that one finds a similar mixture of romantic tone with classical and mythological references. Hölderlin, often dubbed a "premature surrealist," became mad midway through his long life (dying at about 78) and spent the second half of his allotted time on earth (about 40 years) in insanity.

If Hamburger had mentioned Corbiere as an influence, because of Celan's use of an erudite slanginess, I might have agreed with him. He mentions Brecht only to state that Celan is not political. Otherwise there might be a connection there also.

Anyway, avant-garde (big catch-all term) Celan certainly is and, in the world of the avant-garde, apparent contradiction in a man's attitudes and confusion in his biography seems to be a constant. The book was not a pleasure to read; none of the poems will remain in my memory—and $20.00 looms as an absurd, Ubu-esque price to pay for it.

HUNDRED FLOWERS BASEBALL

The Temple of Baseball
Edited by Richard Grossinger

This is a thoroughly sophisticated and up-to-the-moment (1984 season) anthology of baseball pieces, most of which are a great joy to read. The piece I liked best is the one by the anthologist himself, on the Mets, since I have been into the Mets from 1963 on, when somebody said to me that the Mets were the beatniks of baseball. Paeans to America, like Kerouac's, really like Ginsberg's, like Whitman's, somehow intermingle with the baseball-ism and produce "oddities" which are really not oddities, like Sadaharu Oh's piece on Zen and baseball. References in one of the pieces to the Boschian quality of midwestern faces denouncing a player for a baseball miscue evoke for me images of baseball-mad boys wearing baseball caps in mental hospitals like I wrote about in the fifties. Extremely hip sociological insight with a baseball backdrop are the province of most of these contributors who are, in their minds, watching everything from Greek Tragedy to totalitarian rallies beside mere baseball games.

There is a surreal sketch by W.P. Kinsella, about ghastly fans replacing artificial turf with real sod in a stadium during a baseball strike. Strangely enough, this piece reminded me both of early fiction by John Hawkes and recent passages from Stephen King's *Pet Sematary*.

There is a recurrent intertwining of the literary-philosophical and the athletic throughout this anthology which makes it plain that this is not merely a baseball book, but a book about poetry and baseball, or about the poetry of baseball.

For me baseball and fishing are two sports which I have had recourse to throughout my life when I met reverses elsewhere or when I wished to establish some sort of continuity. Baseball is definitely a means of re-capturing contact with the Zeitgeist when you have, as has always been inevitable with me, been thoroughly outdistanced in many areas.

However there is baseball and there is this sort of intellectual approach to baseball. Just as there is fishing, when you fish with nonliterary types, and fishing when you go fishing with Allen Ginsberg in a rowboat at City Island. Others wait patiently for bites while Allen recites haikus about "little silver fish." The literary types inevitably revert to their specialities. What generally emerges, though, is a mingling of corn and erudition.

And to add to the generally stew-like nature of all of this, besides the patriotic Zen-beatnik-Kerouacian types, you also have the Fidelistas and other Marxian types throwing their two cents in. No Russians claiming baseball is a Russian game, anyway. The answer seems to be that anyone can make anything of baseball. Just be American after your own fashion. Like a Maoist "hundred-flowers" kind of Marxism.

Codrescu's piece draws on Freud; Mikhail Horovitz, Tom Clark, Tom Blaess and Debra Heimerdinger contribute visual art which further adds to the grab bag of goodies here enclosed.

It's been a long road for me between the Al Simmons days and the Dwight Gooden days, but I find names and occurrences in this book which remind me of just about every phase anyone my age can recall. Posing as a baseball maven is just a little bit embarrassing to me, because a cousin of mine in the thirties, who was writing sports for the New York *Post* (the pre-Dorothy Schiff New York *Post*), wrote an article referring to me as "The Boy Base-ball Sage of the Bronx." I was 8 then. Kerouac saw this piece and it has been hard to live down.

I suppose Ring Lardner's rawboned, tobacco chew-ing ballplayers were like Ring Lardner and I suppose too that Richard Grossinger's post-structuralist ballplayers are like Richard Grossinger—extremely cholesterol-conscious and other odd up-to-date things. Therefore, though you probably need some college to read this anthology, it can still be characterized as excellent baseball writing.

NOT SUCH POPULIST GUSTATORIES
Two Novels
by Philip Whalen

These two novels are literary artifacts recording the manners, mores, attitudes, and conversation of the beatniks and their enemies, the squares, during the post-war golden age when such types flourished in America. Before supply-side economics were even dreamt of, when marijuana use was equated with people having "communist" tendencies—in short, of a period which one would think had never occurred unless one had encountered artifacts like these.

The first of the two novels, called *You Didn't Even Try*, is partially autobiographical and partly invention. Whalen has never married; but the novel is about the failed marriage of a poet-fuzzy-intellectual like himself. He is never realistic (down-to-earth) enough for the wife. He is always bumbling over some esoteric book or other and she is apparently ambitious and materialistic. They are continually arguing over minor household management matters. The post-war years, as I dimly recall them, were full of marriages of this type—none of which lasted for very long.

The roman à clef factor was always present in beatnik novels and for all I know one or two of these characters may be Gary Snyder (who was a friend of Whalen's) or somebody equally famous. There is an attempt at recreation of the memorable milieu. The characters always

seem to be noshing and the author's knowledge of gourmet vocabulary rivals at the very least Joris-Karl Huys-
man's vocabulary of lapidary terms in *A Rebours*. Certain
writers palp and savor recondite terms and Whalen is
definitely one of these. Everything but the recipes. At
times it gets a bit boring, but one should make allowances
for a tour de force of this kind.

Anatole Broyard once wrote of Kerouac that he ex-
celled in nothing so much as describing a man eating a
can of baked beans. I get a similar impression of Whalen,
though his gustatory tastes are not so populist. The leading character is given to endless introspection and his
hairsplitting, to his inner self, over the nuances of various
phases of existence must be common among longevitied
poets. If a poet, early in his life deals with the very basic
problem of suicide, and then rejects it, there ought to be
a lot of subject matter to concern him during the ensuing
years. At times the protraction of existence or of thought
among poets of this type seems even comic. What else but
a waste of time? But why be genocidal towards poets?

I prefer the second of the two novels, written at a
later date in Japan. There's a lot more action here and
the wit of the characters seems sharper. One factor that
bothered me in both novels is the fact that *all* of the
characters, both male and female, seem to function on
the same intellectual level, as though they were all members of a club resembling a slightly more modest Mensa.
They're all adepts in psychoanalysis, existential philosophy, and "normal" sex. There is something a little too
uniform in their loves and arguments when set up against
the crazy-quilt of real life. But maybe these are the kinds
of people that David Riesman used to write about.

The leading character, again a poet, finds life too
Ubu-esque after "two and three quarter world wars" and
in thinking of Albert Camus, understands his "suicide"
because of being forced to choose "between Karl Barth
and Karl Marx."

The final section of the second novel, *Imaginary Speeches*

for a Brazen Head, is the high point of both books—a marvelous depiction of the short-lived beatnik rage—when the leading character is used as a kind of exhibit-curiosity at North Beach. The prose here becomes dazzling for a number of pages.

It was very common during those arty days for ambitious young writers to park on the doorsteps of established big literary names to profess their admiration for them and to establish a generational link. I remember Ginsberg and Burroughs visiting Céline shortly before the famous doctor passed on and I remember Corso and Bremser dropping in uninvited on Auden. This poet of Whalen's talks of dropping in on Robinson Jeffers. Prefamous beatniks generally made a habit of dropping in on famous lostniks. For a recreation of beatnik theory and practice, one can't beat this second novel.

ON ANTLER'S LAST WORDS

When I first met Antler in 1982 or so, I asked him point-blank and in privacy, "Are you a communist?" His answer was, "No." Of course we all remember that Fidel Castro at one time was vaunted in the American press as a Christian agrarian reformer. Maybe Antler is something like that and one day we'll feel he's duped us. No. I believe him. He hates work and he hates factories but at no point seems to call for or even to envisage expropriating the expropriators. There is something else at work here. Something as peculiar to twentieth-century America as David Riesman's conflict between other-directed and inner-directed types—those motivated by peer loyalties rather than by tradition and vice versa. Antler's main invective is directed against the work ethic:

Perhaps I have never left the factory.
Perhaps I'm made to dream the 16 hours my identity
    flees.
It's the drug in the water that does it, remarkable.
To think I'll work here forever thinking I go home and
    return and do all sorts of things in between,
like writing this poem—
Of course I'm not writing this poem!
I'm on the machine now packaging endless ends of
    aluminum for the tops and bottoms of cans.
Our foreman laughed—"You'll wake up in the middle
    of the night as if you're working. It's so easy you can
    do it in your sleep."

Against this he juxtaposes the play-ethic. He is a
product of the sixties and of the eighties. Spawned by
Ginsberg's poetics as Ginsberg was spawned by Whitman's. Beatnik, Wobbly, or Luddite—he distances himself from the new technology that so seduces many today
and becomes your ANTI-FUTURIST par excellence:

This is the hall big as a football field.
Here are the 24 presses chewing can-lids from hand-fed
    sheets of aluminum.
Here are the 10 minsters chomping poptops nonstop
    into lids scooped into their jaws.
Machines large as locomotives, louder than loudest
    rockgroup explosions,
Screeching so loud you go deaf without earplugs,
where the only way to speak is to gesture,
Or bending to your ear as if I were telling a secret
the yell from my cupped hands less than a whisper.

If Hart Crane was turned on by modern engineering
and the poetry of bridge cables and if Italian futurism
eulogized the century of speed and machines; if Yank,
O'Neill's "Hairy Ape," glorified his power over the engine
that drove the ship; if I was fascinated by the mechanical

marvel of my computerized cash register when I worked in a department store—so does Antler vaunt the human element, the shagginess, the laziness, the sensuality of the human body and so does he damn the streamlined sleek, efficient, unfeeling tyrant: the machine.

He catalogues as Whitman and Ginsberg catalogued. He is perhaps a bit more slavishly Whitmanesque than Ginsberg. And for his cataloguing he has a fresher and more varied, more neologistic vocabulary than the poets he most resembles. He has the language "in his pocket." He is a marvel of virtuosity, with tremendous agility, change of pace, and sense of the dramatic. While "Factory" is a powerful polemical poem, the title poem of the book, "Last Words" bowls you over with a freshness that Ihaven't seen in anything in years and with a talent for the phrase and the *mot juste* that recalls St. John Perse, Claudel, Bloy, and Peguy from the long-line French prose poetic tradition. This is a major American poet.

His attitude toward sex as illustrated in his poem, "Whitmansexual" is just that, an exact programmatic translation of Walt's sexual philosophy into the America of the 1980s. Where do his economic views fit in, where do his ecological and erotic views fit in? His libertarian views of mental health? Of defecation? Everywhere. This is an astonishingly topical and timely book. An articulate contemporary of the punks. Perhaps a big brother to them (Artaud's Big Brother not Orwell's). His virus has the power to activate antibodies. Something which just about everybody now lacks in our sanitized literature. Read Antler, to discover anew the power to surprise, to shock, to awaken.

EXOTIC NIHILISTIC HEDONISM

The Last Museum
by Brion Gysin

Nobody (none of the characters, that is) in this novel by Brion Gysin either works or goes to the bathroom. This is a common characteristic of most modern novels, but the activities of these characters are so extraordinary that the above activities seem beneath mention for such people. None of them are on welfare, none take disability. None belong to unions. In short, they are beyond my ken. Perhaps it is I who am *different*. Yet I feel safe in asserting that one need not fear being perceived as a closet Stalinist by dubbing this work extremely decadent. "The direction of the organism is forward," wrote Harry Stack Sullivan. For Brion Gysin, *forward* meant smoking hashish while surrounded by oxygen tanks and suffering from terminal emphysema-cum-lung cancer. Exotic nihilistic hedonism? To my way of thinking: yes. Insanity? Again yes. But a very debonair, witty, erudite, grammatical kind of insanity—not the kind of seedy, sputum-spattered insanity one sees on the streets of New York.

There is a comradely introduction, a tribute by Gysin's collaborator, William Burroughs. Characters in the novel, like Dr. Benway and Benway's nurse-baboon, are borrowed from *Naked Lunch*. There is enough similarity in the prose styles of various works I have seen by these two friends to indicate a symbiotic literary relationship between the two. This particular work is a satire based on goings-on in the Beat Hotel where the prominant Beats lived as American expatriates in mid-fifties Paris. Here the name is changed to the "Bardo" hotel (Bards—get it?). Among the characters is the fabulous Sheree, who is the rumored murderess (specifically, poisoner) of the equally fabulous Jane Bowles, wife of the composer-novelist Paul Bowles, referred to in the *Voice* as "the kike dyke."

I worked in a bookstore in the early eighties where an alcoholic, chain-smoking public relations person scheduled Jane Bowles for a reading from her work despite the fact that Jane Bowles was known to have been poisoned at least two years earlier.

This is a fitting background for the action of the novel which is high farce on all cylinders, despite being only occasionally humorous and often being, I think, overdone.

This novel, a Beat *Salammbô*, comes to me in my own psychic realm, where I am trapped between post-structuralist mobs and herds of microcephalics. I am most stricken by Gysin smoking hashish while in the throes of emphysema. To me, a brother-emphysemiac who stopped smoking *anything* immediately after diagnosis, a breath of clear, fresh air transcends *all* the wit in the world. But then, my kick is longevity.

IT'S NOT JUST TYPING

The Spontaneous Poetics of Jack Kerouac
by Regina Weinreich

As a onetime editor of Kerouac (during the *On The Road* agony), I am deeply indebted to Regina Weinreich for a critical exposition of Kerouac's method of creation that reveals merit and genius where I and some of my onetime publishing colleagues saw only perversity and novelistic malingering. "It's not writing. It's typing." So it seems, and so *Finnegan's Wake* must have seemed without a skeleton key. Regina Weinreich has written a critical work on Kerouac that is without peer. It is not a lurid biographical work like the spate that have appeared. (I personally breathed a sigh of relief at not having been mentioned in it.) William Burroughs' approval quoted on the dust jacket emphasizes this point also.

Kerouac is here revealed as an extremely hermetic writer who cannot be read on the level of a popular novel as, for example, Camus could be with his James M. Cain technique on the surface level of *The Stranger*. Kerouac now seems to me, because of the wealth of Weinreich's erudition and critical genius, extremely hard reading and with greater proximity to Mallarmé or Valery or, perhaps, to Joyce than to the more accessible writers of his own and other generations. Weinreich makes comparison to Wolfe and to Whitman. But what is clear is that we are not dealing with a mere novelist (though she makes comparison to Balzac and Proust too) but with a prose poet and a mystic. No wonder the publishing world has never and still does not know exactly what to make of him. He was a "novelist" who had the temerity (really worthy of Kit Smart) to a tell a TV interviewer who asked what "beat" meant—"to see the face of God." This was the historical meaning of "beatitude" anyway.

What Weinreich reveals is that in Kerouac we find a focal point of both art and alienation. In him as in perhaps no other American artist of our time.

I would urge a close reading of this critical work upon all of those who have dwelt, like Norman Podhoretz only recently, on whether or not Kerouac was a good role-model to the young. Podhoretz' evaluation, like my own in the past, like Capote's, and like so many others I have heard over the years, is an expedient evasion of the mystery in Kerouac's appeal that has remained unsolved over all these years. Regina's work explores the crevices and inner workings of the mystery—Jack's creative imagination—as nobody to my knowledge (save perhaps Ginsberg) has done up to this point. The reward to anybody still interested in modern literature (book prices being what they are) is enormous.

In actuality what she has done is to divide the novels into major and minor, arranging them both aesthetically and chronologically, connecting them both in terms of Kerouac's personal history and in terms of "outer" history and binding them together according to the laws of his artistic logic. The sequence in the seven critical chapters is intellectual and that alone.

Kerouac, thank God, was not an Errol Flynn and Regina takes him out of that category entirely by telling the reader *nothing new* about Jack's love life.

As a role-model, he emerges as a great novelist. What's wrong with some kid wanting to be a great novelist?—as Jack himself probably wanted to be one day.

Weinreich's book sounds the death-knell of the simplistic explanations of Kerouac's appeal that have sufficied over the years.

What she has done with the apparently simple *bildungsroman, The Town and the City,* is the best demonstration of her critical powers. She uncovers level upon level of deeper meaning here in a chapter entitled *The Brothers Martin Or The Decline of America* and reveals Kerouac (in his first book) as a social critic as caustic as any of his time.

And as a great blessing to a formerly mystified reader of Kerouac's unpunctuated "spontaneous prose"—she supplies a highly credible rationale of that too.

True to its title, this book is more a close examination of the "poetics" of Kerouac's sentences than it is an accumulation of plots. I read it in one sitting and, if you'll excuse me for sounding Rex Reedish, I found it thrilling.